Introducing Issues with Opposing Viewpoints®

Physician-Assisted Suicide

M. M. Eboch, Book Editor

Greenhaven Publishing

Published in 2021 by Greenhaven Publishing, LLC
353 3rd Avenue, Suite 255, New York, NY 10010

First Edition

Articles in Greenhaven Publishing anthologies are often edited for length to meet page requirements. In addition, original titles of these works are changed to clearly present the main thesis and to explicitly indicate the author's opinion. Every effort is made to ensure that Greenhaven Publishing accurately reflects the original intent of the authors. Every effort has been made to trace the owners of the copyrighted material.

Library of Congress Cataloging-in-Publication Data

Names: Eboch, M. M., editor.
Title: Physician-assisted suicide / M. M. Eboch, book editor.
Description: First edition. | New York : Greenhaven Publishing, 2021. | Series: Introducing issues with opposing viewpoints | Includes bibliographical references and index. | Audience: Grades 7–12.
Identifiers: LCCN 2019056487 | ISBN 9781534507159 (library binding) | ISBN 9781534507142 (paperback)
Subjects: LCSH: Assisted suicide—Juvenile literature.
Classification: LCC R726 .P4926 2021 | DDC 179.7—dc23
LC record available at https://lccn.loc.gov/2019056487

Manufactured in the United States of America

Website: http://greenhavenpublishing.com

Contents

Foreword

Indulging in a wide spectrum of ideas, beliefs, and perspectives is a critical cornerstone of democracy. After all, it is often debates over differences of opinion, such as whether to legalize abortion, how to treat prisoners, or when to enact the death penalty, that shape our society and drive it forward. Such diversity of thought is frequently regarded as the hallmark of a healthy and civilized culture. As the Reverend Clifford Schutjer of the First Congregational Church in Mansfield, Ohio, declared in a 2001 sermon, "Surrounding oneself with only like-minded people, restricting what we listen to or read only to what we find agreeable is irresponsible. Refusing to entertain doubts once we make up our minds is a subtle but deadly form of arrogance." With this advice in mind, Introducing Issues with Opposing Viewpoints books aim to open readers' minds to the critically divergent views that comprise our world's most important debates.

Introducing Issues with Opposing Viewpoints simplifies for students the enormous and often overwhelming mass of material now available via print and electronic media. Collected in every volume is an array of opinions that captures the essence of a particular controversy or topic. Introducing Issues with Opposing Viewpoints books embody the spirit of nineteenth-century journalist Charles A. Dana's axiom: "Fight for your opinions, but do not believe that they contain the whole truth, or the only truth." Absorbing such contrasting opinions teaches students to analyze the strength of an argument and compare it to its opposition. From this process readers can inform and strengthen their own opinions, or be exposed to new information that will change their minds. Introducing Issues with Opposing Viewpoints is a mosaic of different voices. The authors are statesmen, pundits, academics, journalists, corporations, and ordinary people who have felt compelled to share their experiences and ideas in a public forum. Their words have been collected from newspapers, journals, books, speeches, interviews, and the Internet, the fastest growing body of opinionated material in the world.

Introducing Issues with Opposing Viewpoints shares many of the well-known features of its critically acclaimed parent series, Opposing

Viewpoints. The articles allow readers to absorb and compare divergent perspectives. Active reading questions preface each viewpoint, requiring the student to approach the material thoughtfully and carefully. Photographs, charts, and graphs supplement each article. A thorough introduction provides readers with crucial background on an issue. An annotated bibliography points the reader toward articles, books, and websites that contain additional information on the topic. An appendix of organizations to contact contains a wide variety of charities, nonprofit organizations, political groups, and private enterprises that each hold a position on the issue at hand. Finally, a comprehensive index allows readers to locate content quickly and efficiently.

Introducing Issues with Opposing Viewpoints is also significantly different from Opposing Viewpoints. As the series title implies, its presentation will help introduce students to the concept of opposing viewpoints and learn to use this material to aid in critical writing and debate. The series' four-color, accessible format makes the books attractive and inviting to readers of all levels. In addition, each viewpoint has been carefully edited to maximize a reader's understanding of the content. Short but thorough viewpoints capture the essence of an argument. A substantial, thought-provoking essay question placed at the end of each viewpoint asks the student to further investigate the issues raised in the viewpoint, compare and contrast two authors' arguments, or consider how one might go about forming an opinion on the topic at hand. Each viewpoint contains sidebars that include at-a-glance information and handy statistics. A Facts About section located in the back of the book further supplies students with relevant facts and figures.

Following in the tradition of the Opposing Viewpoints series, Greenhaven Publishing continues to provide readers with invaluable exposure to the controversial issues that shape our world. As John Stuart Mill once wrote: "The only way in which a human being can make some approach to knowing the whole of a subject is by hearing what can be said about it by persons of every variety of opinion and studying all modes in which it can be looked at by every character of mind. No wise man ever acquired his wisdom in any mode but this." It is to this principle that Introducing Issues with Opposing Viewpoints books are dedicated.

Introduction

"If they are facing a slow, painful death, Americans want options. Many believe that asking for help in dying is a moral option. They don't believe that suffering until they die of natural causes is the only way out."

—Scott McConnell, executive director of LifeWay Research

Death with dignity … assisted suicide … medical aid in dying … euthanasia. All may refer to people choosing to die before a terminal illness kills them, and doctors helping with this choice. The many terms used reflect the wide views people have on this subject.

Different people and organizations use these different terms. Several medical societies oppose the terms *suicide* or *assisted suicide* to describe the practice of medical professionals helping people die. They may prefer the terms *physician-assisted death* or *medical aid-in-dying*. These terms feel neutral and more clinical.

Public groups that support legalizing the practice often call it death with dignity. This puts a positive spin on the practice by focusing on allowing the patient to choose how they end their life. Many of the laws supporting physician-assisted death are called "death with dignity" laws.

Those opposed to the practice may call it *physician-assisted suicide, suicide*, or *euthanasia*. Those terms evoke the negative emotions many people have about suicide and euthanasia. Many religions consider suicide a sin. People often associate euthanasia with killing someone without their knowledge or permission. Using these terms can immediately create negative feelings.

Compassion and Choices is a nonprofit organization in favor of "individual choice at the end of life, including access to medical aid in dying." According to them, "Euthanasia is an intentional act by which another person (not the dying person) administers the medication. By contrast, medical aid in dying requires the patient to be able to take the medication themselves and therefore always remain in control." By these definitions, the only difference is in whether the dying person takes the drug themselves, or the physician administers an injection. In both cases, the patient's wishes should be followed.

Laws may also address these terms. Medical aid-in-dying laws often state that "Actions taken in accordance with [the Act] shall not, for any purpose, constitute suicide, assisted suicide, mercy killing or homicide."

Does the name of the practice really matter? It might if you are trying to influence people. A 2018 Gallup poll found that 72 percent of Americans support physician-assisted death. That's when the question was asked like this: "When a person has a disease that cannot be cured, do you think doctors should be allowed by law to end the patient's life by some painless means if the patient and his or her family request it?"

On the other hand, support dropped when the question was asked like this: "When a person has a disease that cannot be cured and is living in severe pain, do you think doctors should or should not be allowed by law to assist the patient to commit suicide if the patient requests it?" In that case, 65 percent of respondents said yes.

The first question describes euthanasia, where someone else administers the fatal drug. That is illegal in the United States. The second question describes doctor-assisted suicide, where the patient is in control of taking a fatal dose of medication. That is legal in a few states. Why would people think it's all right for a doctor to kill someone, but not for the patient to kill themselves? Does it really matter who administers the medicine? Perhaps some people heard the word "suicide" and felt that it must always be wrong.

These questions show how much emotion plays into public opinion about physician-assisted death. On the one hand, many people believe that a terminally ill person who is suffering has a right to choose how their life ends. On the other hand, many people believe that suicide and murder are always wrong.

In addition, some groups worry that legalizing physician-assisted death could have unintended consequences. Will insurance companies pressure doctors to recommend death instead of expensive treatments that might extend life? Will people be forced to choose death because they cannot afford their medical care? The practice is supposed to relieve suffering. Finances shouldn't enter into it—but it's not hard to imagine a time when they might.

When it comes to ending suffering, is physician-assisted death the best method? Pain can usually be relieved through medication. Mental anguish might be lessened through counseling. Palliative care is specialized medical care designed to treat pain and stress in patients with serious illnesses. Unfortunately, it is not widely practiced. Some patients may not have the option or may not know the option exists. Would it be better to expand palliative care rather than legalize physician-assisted death?

Society would surely benefit by the widespread use of palliative care. Financial issues could be lessened by making healthcare available to everyone for little or no cost. These responses would be expensive, but they would help people at the ends of their lives. Will society ever be willing to pay the cost?

Regardless, some people argue that death should always be a choice for terminally ill people. Some may not want to spend their last months in a hospital bed. They may feel that life is not worth living if they cannot take care of themselves or do things they enjoy. They may see no point in waiting around for death. "Death with dignity" laws are designed to give these people an option.

The question remains, will it always be the patient's choice? Laws are written with language designed to prevent abuse. Typically they require a patient to be a mentally-competent adult. They must have a terminal illness and a life expectancy of no more than six months. They must voluntarily request medication to hasten their inevitable death. Two physicians must confirm that these things are true. Waiting periods give the patient time to change their mind.

Still, opposition groups claim that abuse can and does happen. Some cases in which insurance companies encouraged doctors to recommend physician-assisted death have been reported.

In the United States, mental illness alone is not an acceptable reason for physician-assisted death. In other countries, it can be. This means that physically healthy young adults may choose to end their lives with a doctor's help. Will that someday be true in the

United States? People with physical and mental disabilities often feel unwanted. Will legalizing physician-assisted death lead to doctors or family members pressuring them to choose death?

The situation grows even more complicated when dealing with dementia. What if a mentally-competent patient asks to die once their disease progresses, yet as the dementia becomes more severe, they change their mind? Which choice should be followed?

Physician-assisted death is surrounded by controversy. Is it a danger to society? Does it allow people freedom and dignity at the end of their lives? Exploring the issues through research, philosophical discussions, and personal experience can help individuals determine their answer. The current debates are explored in *Introducing Issues with Opposing Viewpoints: Physician-Assisted Suicide*, shedding light on this ongoing contemporary issue.

Chapter 1

Who Supports Physician-Assisted Suicide?

Supporters of physician-assisted suicide protest in front of the US Supreme Court.

Viewpoint 1

Views of Suicide Have Changed Throughout History

"For more than 700 years, common-law tradition has opposed and punished both suicide and actively assisting or encouraging suicide."

Ian Macleod

In the following viewpoint, Ian Macleod responds to a law that legalized physician-assisted death in Canada. The author traces some of the background to physician-assisted suicide, in Canada and worldwide. He notes that in antiquity, committing suicide was acceptable and sometimes even seen as honorable. Some early Christians committed suicide in the hopes of reaching salvation. Over time, many religions and governments came to see suicide as a form of murder. More recently, society started to see suicide as a symptom of disease. Ian Macleod writes for *Ottawa Citizen*, a newspaper in Ontario, Canada.

"A Short History of Assisted Suicide," by Ian Macleod, Postmedia Network Inc, January 10, 2016. Reprinted by permission.

AS YOU READ, CONSIDER THE FOLLOWING QUESTIONS:

1. How have attitudes about suicide and physician-assisted death changed over time?
2. How did Christianity change its views of suicide over time? Why?
3. How did suicide become associated with murder?

As government scrambles to legislate around last year's Supreme Court of Canada judgment decriminalizing physician-assisted death, reaching political consensus will be tough. The right-to-die debate has been one of the most tempestuous ethical clashes of the past quarter-century in Canada.

Over the ages, western civilization has both honoured and condemned voluntary death. Now public, legal and political opinion is shifting to a delicate, some say dangerous, new ground that will revisit and challenge age-old attitudes.

Last February's Supreme Court ruling limits physician-assisted suicide to competent adults who clearly consent to end their life, and have incurable, but not necessarily terminal, medical conditions that cause "intolerable" physical or psychological pain.

The trick now is to quickly craft a law reflecting that.

On Monday, lawyers for the federal and some provincial governments will appear before the court and ask for a six-month suspension of the court's Feb. 6 deadline when the existing and impugned Criminal Code law against assisted suicide becomes constitutionally invalid.

Western culture, at least until recently, never condoned acts of suicide, assisted or not. But over the past four centuries, society has very slowly come to view and respond to self-destruction, and now assisted suicide, much differently. Canada, for example, decriminalized the act of attempted suicide in 1972.

Until last year's court ruling, however, assisted suicide remained a crime, punishable by up to 14 years in prison. That meant severely infirm individuals physically incapable of legally killing themselves did not have the same life-ending option as suffering but able-bodied individuals.

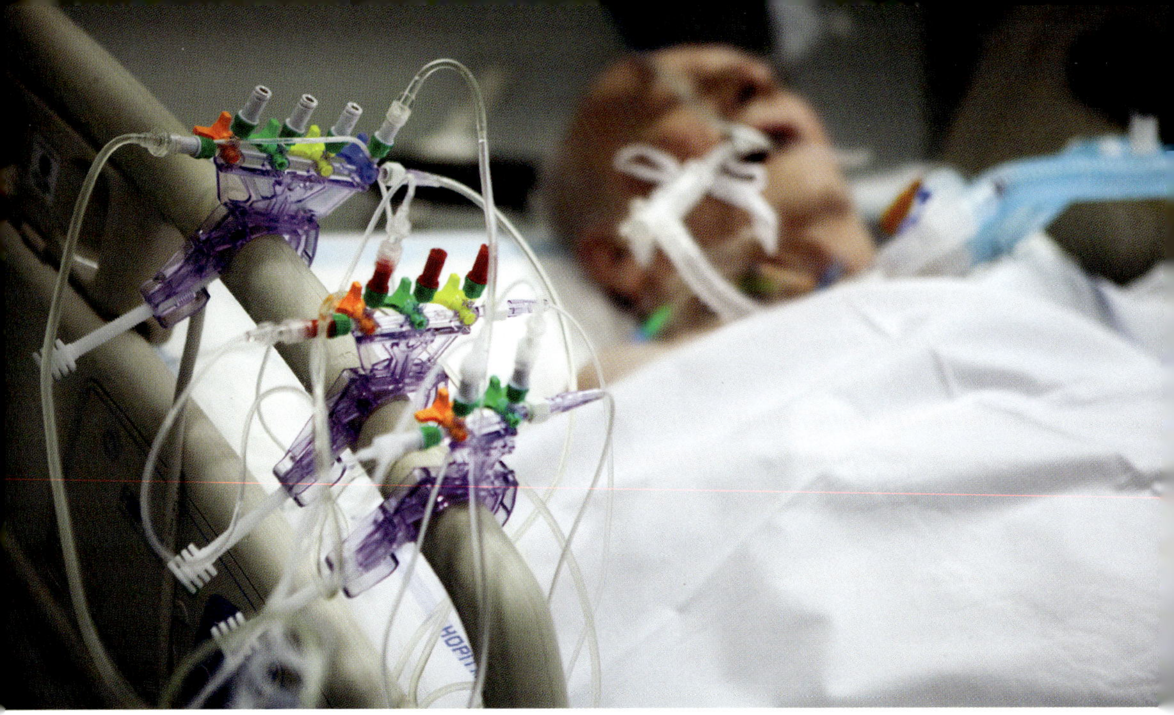

Opinions about voluntary death have changed over time. Once considered honorable, suicide and assisted suicide are now more commonly believed to be morally wrong and legally criminal.

Such was the plight of Sue Rodriguez, a 43-year-old Victoria woman living with amyotrophic lateral sclerosis (ALS), Lou Gehrig's disease. She appealed to the Supreme Court in 1993 for the right to a doctor-assisted death, arguing the law violated her Section 7 Charter right, which, in her view, included the right to control the method, timing and circumstances of death.

The court, in a 5-4 decision, disagreed. It found the law criminalizing assisted suicide did not infringe on her constitutional right to "life, liberty and security of the person" and said the law existed to protect the most vulnerable, namely the frail elderly, the disabled, the mentally ill and the impoverished.

Rodriguez killed herself anyway, with the help of an anonymous doctor. And 22 years later, last Feb. 6, the Supreme Court finally agreed that doctors can legally help others die.

With the legal pendulum in motion again, it's instructive to look at the often contradictory history of attitudes on suicide, assisted suicide and other forms of voluntary death.

Depending on the century, voluntary death has been considered honourable and heroic, an act of faith, an act of treason, a sin, a political protest, the devil's work or a sign of madness.

For more than 700 years, common-law tradition has opposed and punished both suicide and actively assisting or encouraging suicide.

Passive euthanasia, generally considered the deliberate withdrawal or withholding of medical treatment from the terminally ill, also was seen as wrong, as was active euthanasia, usually involving giving a consenting person suffering unbearably an overdose of muscle relaxants or sedatives causing a coma and then death.

Various forms of euthanasia and assisted suicide for the terminally or hopelessly ill have been sanctioned over the past 20 years in Holland, Belgium, Luxembourg, Colombia and Albania. Switzerland pioneered assisted suicide law in 1942.

The United States Supreme Court ruled in 1997 that Americans do not have a constitutional right to doctor-assisted dying. But in 2006 the court said individual states could decide for themselves. Physician-assisted suicide is now legal in four states and under consideration in several others.

The changing attitudes, which mirror the advance of modern medical knowledge, technology and palliative care, is a move back toward the thinking—but for far different reasons—of classical antiquity. In ancient Greece and imperial Rome, for example, assisted suicide was common and tolerated.

They "did not think that all human life had inherent values," according to *A Concise History of Euthanasia* by Ian Dowbigging. Sparta, he writes, graphically demonstrates the extremes to which the ancient Greek toleration of self-destruction could lead.

Newborns deemed "feeble and ill-shaped" were put to death as a way of protecting society from the unnecessary burden (and, according to other scholars, "save" the child from the burden of existence).

The ancient Greeks also not only condoned the suicide of people suffering extreme pain and incurable illness, but did not stop physicians from doling out poison. Even Plato, whose reasoning influenced centuries of philosophy and political thinking, believed: "Mentally and physically ill persons should be left to death; they do not have the right to live."

Suicide as a way of expressing a higher ideal also abounds in classical antiquity: Socrates, Lucretia, Cato, Portia, Brutus, Cassius, Seneca, Antony and Cleopatra. (It later inspired the literary tragedies of Ophelia, Othello, Romeo and Juliet, Dante's Seventh Circle of Hell and art by Rembrandt, Titian, Bruegel, Warhol and others.)

The Hippocratic body of writings was the first clear denunciation of mercy killing and assisted suicide in western medical history. For different reasons, the practices were later outlawed by many organized religions—Christianity, Islam, Judaism and Hinduism—and then by the state.

The Bible does not explicitly condemn suicide and includes such Old Testament deaths as those of Abimelech, Samson and Saul, and the New Testament's hanging of Judas Iscariot.

Voluntary death as an act of faith was so embraced by early Christians as a way of reaching their eternal salvation that church leaders became concerned about the number of martyrs—notably the Donatists—departing the church's control.

The church fiercely opposed the Donatists flinging themselves off cliffs. St. Augustine, in The City of God, decreed suicide to be an unpardonable sin that violated the commandment "Thou shall not murder."

His recasting of suicide as murder, as opposed to the Roman ideal of heroic individualism, came at a time when the church was consolidating its hold over its followers. What made suicide a sin was its voluntary nature, seen as a deliberate challenge to divine authority.

Centuries later, Catholic theologian and philosopher St. Thomas Aquinas issued a similarly influential condemnation of suicide as a mortal sin in his theological masterpiece, Summa Theologica. (He, too, distinguished between suicide and martyrdom.)

In the sixth century, St. Augustine's theological arguments on suicide became canon law and burial rites were denied to Christians who killed themselves.

By the Middle Ages, an anti-suicide/mercy killing attitude swept the West, reflected in religious doctrines, secular literature and law. Suicide became not only a violation against God, but a criminal act under common law in England in the 10th century, and a crime throughout medieval Europe.

It was viewed as the ultimate act of non-confidence in a ruler and, since individuals were subjects of the state, even an act of rebellion. So it was treated much like murder. Those who attempted suicide were imprisoned and some, incredibly, were executed.

Fast Fact

Canada made assisted dying legal in June of 2016. The law governs who is eligible. For one thing, it is available only to residents eligible for Canadian health care coverage. This is intended to prevent people from traveling to Canada for access to assisted suicide.

Public attitudes in the west toward self-destruction began changing during the Renaissance. In 1600, Shakespeare penned Hamlet's timeless "To be, or not to be?" soliloquy. By the late 16th century, English law began to excuse suicide if the severity of a physical illness could be demonstrated, or if the person was too young or too mad to understand the consequences.

The Enlightenment of the 17th and 18th centuries brought more questioning. In 1783, David Hume, the British philosopher and historian, caused an uproar in Europe with his Essays on Suicide and the Immortality of the Soul. He argued suicide was morally acceptable and, if ending one's life was an offence to God, so was extending one's life beyond its natural course.

During the French Revolution, some sans-culottes turned suicide into an act of political protest, a defiant affirmation of liberty and personal freedom. After the revolution, France became the first country to decriminalize suicide and attempted suicide. Early French psychiatrists started evaluating it, not in terms of morality but as a product of mental illness.

Suicide slowly moved into the realm of disease, a product of melancholy and the depersonalization of an increasingly industrialized world. Suicidal thoughts were considered the extreme result of untreated physical imbalances in the body, such as fever and constipation.

Through the 20th century, suicide became the realm of sociologists, psychiatrists, psychologists, psychoanalysts and neurobiologists, all with competing theories and therapies. Initial pressure for allowing assisted suicide in the U.S. is credited to the eugenics movement in the early years of the last century.

In 1998, the CBS newsmagazine, *60 Minutes*, showed Michigan pathologist Jack "Doctor Death" Kevorkian and his "Mercitron" suicide machine administering a lethal injection to Thomas Youk, a 52-year-old man suffering from ALS. Kevorkian, who said he assisted in more than 130 deaths, was convicted and sentenced to a 10- to 25-year sentence for murder.

By 2007, polls suggested a strong majority of Canadians believed doctor-assisted suicide for terminally ill patients should be legal.

EVALUATING THE AUTHOR'S ARGUMENTS:

In this viewpoint Ian Macleod explains that people have had complex and changing views of suicide and physician-assisted death over the centuries. How do you currently feel about the arguments regarding physician-assisted death? Why?

Viewpoint 2

Doctors Should Not Help People Die

"For some of these physicians, the process of participating in physician-assisted suicide exacted a large emotional toll."

Ronald W. Pies

In the following viewpoint Dr. Ronald W. Pies considers the ethics of medical decisions. He notes that a majority of doctors favor legal physician-assisted death. However, those doctors who participate in helping people die sometimes regret their actions. Helping patients die can take a great emotional toll on physicians. The author also argues that helping people die goes against the Hippocratic oath. This ancient oath set out ethics guidelines for physicians. Most doctors today do not swear to the original Hippocratic oath, but many do take an oath when they graduate from medical school. Ronald W. Pies is a clinical professor of psychiatry at Tufts University and lecturer on psychiatry at Harvard Medical School.

AS YOU READ, CONSIDER THE FOLLOWING QUESTIONS:

1. How do most doctors feel about physician-assisted death?
2. Why do most people choose physician-assisted suicide (PAS)?
3. How do doctors feel after helping people end their lives?

When my mother was in her final months, suffering from a heart failure and other problems, she called me to her bedside with a pained expression. She took my hand and asked plaintively, "How do I get out of this mess?"

As a physician, I dreaded the question that might follow: Would I help her end her life by prescribing a lethal drug?

Fortunately for me, my mother tolerated her final weeks at home, with the help of hospice nurses and occasional palliative medication. She never raised the thorny question of what is variously termed "medical aid in dying" or "physician-assisted suicide."

As a son and family member who has witnessed the difficult final days of parents and loved ones, I can understand why support for MAID/PAS is growing among the general public. But as a physician and medical ethicist, I believe that MAID/PAS flies in the face of a 2,000-year imperative of Hippocratic medicine: "Do no harm to the patient."

Studies point out that even many doctors who actually participate in MAID/PAS remain uneasy or "conflicted" about it. In this piece, I explore their ambivalence.

Assisted Suicides

In discussing end-of-life issues, both the general public and physicians themselves need to distinguish three different approaches.

MAID/PAS involves a physician's providing the patient with a prescription of a lethal drug that the patient could take anytime to end life. In contrast, active euthanasia or "mercy killing" involves causing the death of a person, typically through a lethal injection given by a physician. Finally, the term "passive euthanasia" refers to hastening the death of a terminally ill person by removing some vital form of support. An example would be disconnecting a respirator.

Increasing International Acceptance

In the U.S. some form of legislatively approved MAID/PAS (but not active euthanasia) is legal in five states and the District of Columbia. In my home state—following a passionate debate—the Massachusetts Medical Society recently decided to rescind its long-held opposition

Many physicians—even those who participate in it—are often conflicted about the issue of medical aid in dying.

to the practice. MMS has taken a position of "neutral engagement," which it claims will allow it to "serve as a medical and scientific resource … that will support shared decision making between terminally ill patients and their trusted physicians."

In a few countries, MAID/PAS has grown increasingly common. In Canada, for example, MAID/PAS was legalized in 2016. In Belgium and the Netherlands, both active euthanasia and physician-assisted suicide are permitted by law, even for patients whose illnesses may be treatable, as with major depression; and whose informed consent may be compromised, as in Alzheimer's disease. In the Netherlands, a proposed "Completed Life Bill" would allow any persons age 75 or over who decide their life is "complete" to be euthanized—even if the person is otherwise healthy.

U.S. Physician Response

Among U.S. physicians, MAID/PAS remains controversial, but national data point to its increasing acceptance. A report published in December 2016 found 57 percent of doctors agreed that physician-assisted death should be available to the terminally ill—up from

> **FAST FACT**
>
> ***Medical aid in dying* (*MAID*), *physician-assisted death*, and *physician-assisted suicide* (*PAS*) are different terms for the same thing. They involve a physician prescribing a lethal drug that a patient could take to end life.**

54 percent in 2014 and 46 percent in 2010.

Perhaps this trend is not surprising. After all, what sort of physician would want to deny dying patients the option of ending their suffering and avoiding an agonizing, painful death?

But this question is misleading. Most persons requesting PAS are not actively experiencing extreme suffering or inadequate pain control. Data from the Washington and Oregon PAS programs show that most patients choose PAS because they fear loss of dignity and control over their own lives.

Some Physicians Feel Conflicted

Physicians who carry out assisted suicide have a wide variety of emotional and psychological responses. In a structured, in-depth telephone interview survey of 38 U.S. oncologists who reported participating in euthanasia or PAS, more than half of the physicians received "comfort" from having carried out euthanasia or PAS.

"Comfort" was not explicitly defined, but, for example, these physicians felt that they had helped patients end their lives in the way the patients wished. However, nearly a quarter of the physicians regretted their actions. Another 16 percent reported that the emotional burden of performing euthanasia or PAS adversely affected their medical practice.

For example, one physician felt so "burned out" that he moved from the city in which he was practicing to a small town.

Other data support the observation that MAID/PAS can be emotionally disturbing to the physician.

Kenneth R. Stevens Jr., an emeritus professor at Oregon Health and Science University, reported that for some physicians in Oregon, participation in PAS was very stressful. For example, in 1998, the first year of Oregon's "Death with Dignity Act," 14 physicians wrote prescriptions for lethal medications for the 15 patients who died from physician-assisted suicide.

The state's annual 1998 report observed that:

> *For some of these physicians, the process of participating in physician-assisted suicide exacted a large emotional toll, as reflected by such comments as, "It was an excruciating thing to do … it made me rethink life's priorities," "This was really hard on me, especially being there when he took the pills," and "This had a tremendous emotional impact."*

Similarly, reactions among European doctors suggest that PAS and euthanasia often provoke strong negative feelings.

Why the Discomfort?

As a physician and medical ethicist, I am opposed to any form of physician assistance with a patient's suicide. Furthermore, I believe that the term "medical aid in dying" allows physicians to avoid the harsh truth that they are helping patients kill themselves. This is also the view of the very influential American College of Physicians.

I believe that the ambivalence and discomfort experienced by a substantial percentage of PAS-participating physicians is directly connected to the Hippocratic Oath—arguably, the most important foundational document in medical ethics. The Oath clearly states:

> *I will neither give a deadly drug to anybody if asked for it, nor will I make a suggestion to this effect.*

In 5th century BC Greece, Hippocrates was something of a revolutionary in this respect. As the classicist and medical historian, Ludwig Edelstein has pointed out some non-Hippocratic physicians probably did provide poisons to their dying patients, in order to spare them protracted suffering. Hippocrates opposed this practice, though he did not believe that terminally ill patients should be exposed to unnecessary and futile medical treatment.

Palliative care specialist Ira Byock has observed that:

> *From its very inception, the profession of medicine has formally prohibited its members from using their special*

knowledge to cause death or harm to others. This was—and is—a necessary protection so that the power of medicine is not used against vulnerable people.

Indeed, when patients nearing the end of life express fears of losing control, or being deprived of dignity, compassionate and supportive counseling is called for—not assistance in committing suicide.

To be sure, comprehensive palliative care, including home hospice nursing, should be provided to the subset of terminally ill patients who require pain relief. But as physician and ethicist Leon Kass has put it:

We must care for the dying, not make them dead.

EVALUATING THE AUTHOR'S ARGUMENTS:

This viewpoint argues that helping patients end their lives is emotionally hard on doctors. Should doctors avoid ever harming patients, even if the patient is at the end of their life and suffering? Or do doctors have a responsibility to help people end their lives the way they wish? Should the suffering of doctors be taken into account when laws and guidelines about physician-assisted death are considered?

Viewpoint 3

Most People Support Legal Physician-Assisted Death

"If they are facing a slow, painful death, Americans want options. Many believe that asking for help in dying is a moral option."

Bob Smietana

In the following viewpoint, Bob Smietana examines public opinion on physician-assisted death. He notes that the majority of Americans believe terminally ill patients should be able to ask for a doctor's help in ending their lives. Different demographic groups may have different views. Yet most people across groups support legal physician-assisted death. Nones, or those with no religious affiliation, are among the most likely to support it. People with evangelical beliefs, which are usually associated with born-again Christians, are least likely to support physician-assisted death. Bob Smietana is editor in chief at Religion News Service.

AS YOU READ, CONSIDER THE FOLLOWING QUESTIONS:

1. What percentage of people believe that it is morally acceptable to ask for a physician's aid in taking one's own life?
2. Do age or race make a difference in whether people support legal physician-assisted death?
3. How does religion influence views on physician-assisted death?

"Most Americans Say Assisted Suicide Is Morally Acceptable," by Bob Smietana, LifeWay, December 6, 2016. Reprinted by permission.

The American Medical Association has described physician-assisted suicide as a serious risk to society and "fundamentally incompatible with a physician's role as healer." Millions of Americans disagree.

Two-thirds say it is morally acceptable for terminally ill patients to ask their doctors for help in ending their lives, according to a new survey from Nashville-based LifeWay Research. A similar number says doctors should be able to help terminally ill patients die.

Scott McConnell, executive director of LifeWay Research, says Americans want more say over how they die. That's especially true if facing a painful, terminal illness, he says.

"If they are facing a slow, painful death, Americans want options," he says. "Many believe that asking for help in dying is a moral option. They don't believe that suffering until they die of natural causes is the only way out."

Widespread Support

Physician-assisted suicide first became legal in the U.S. in 1997 under Oregon's "Death with Dignity" law. Since then, 991 patients in Oregon have ended their lives using medications prescribed by a doctor under the law, according to that state's reports.

Today six states allow physician-assisted suicide. The latest is Colorado, where voters approved Proposition 106, which allows a terminally ill patient to request a fatal dose of sleeping medication, by a two-to-one margin in November. Washington, California, Vermont, and Montana also allow physician-assisted suicide. The city council in the District of Columbia recently approved a measure allowing the practice—a decision that must be reviewed by Congress.

In LifeWay Research's survey, 67 percent of Americans agree with the statement, "When a person is facing a painful terminal disease, it is morally acceptable to ask for a physician's aid in taking his or her own life." Thirty-three percent disagree.

Where there are differences among demographic groups, most still agree. For example, Americans age 18 to 24 (77 percent) and those 35 to 44 (63 percent) and 55 to 64 (64 percent) agree. So do white Americans (71 percent) and Hispanic Americans (69 percent). Those with some college education (71 percent) or with graduate

Americans' Support for Legal Doctor-Assisted Suicide

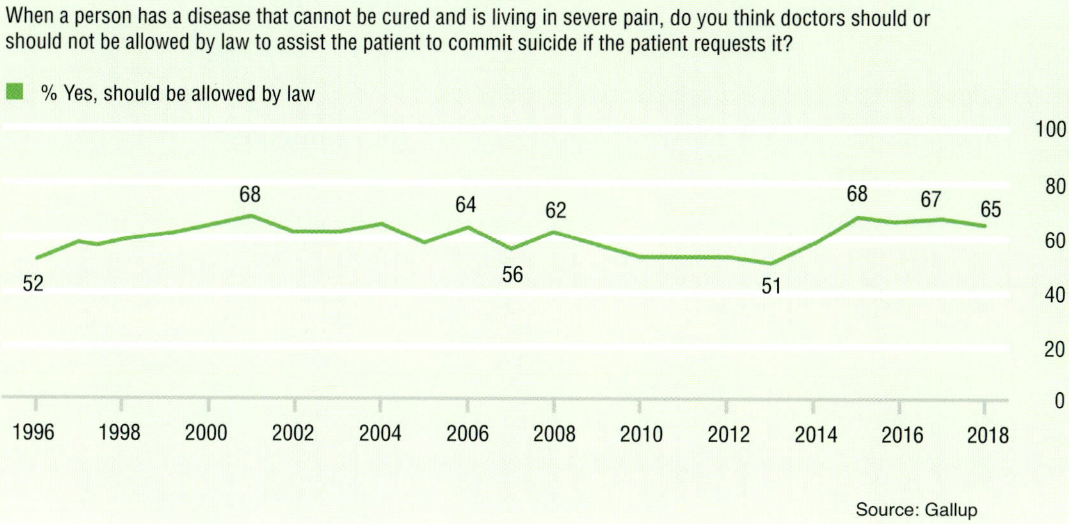

On average, support for physician-assisted suicide in the United States has grown over the past quarter century.

degrees (73 percent) and those with high school diplomas or less (61 percent) also agree.

Among faith groups, more than half of all Christians (59 percent), Catholics (70 percent), Protestants (53 percent), Nones (84 percent) and those of other religions (70 percent) agree. Most of those who attend religious services less than once a month (76 percent) also agree.

A few demographic groups are skeptical. Fewer than half of those with evangelical beliefs (38 percent), African-Americans (47 percent) or those who attend religious services at least once a month (49 percent) say physician-assisted suicide is morally acceptable.

"Traditional Christian teaching says God holds the keys to life and death," says McConnell. "Those who go

Fast Fact

In 2018, Gallup reported, "While support for legalized euthanasia is strong across nearly all subgroups of Americans, men, young adults, Democrats and liberals are especially likely to favor it. Support drops below a majority only among weekly churchgoers."

to church or hold more traditional beliefs are less likely to see assisted suicide as morally acceptable. Still, a surprising number do."

Few Want Restrictions on Doctors

Researchers also found widespread support for removing restrictions on physician-assisted suicide.

Many Americans (69 percent) say physicians should be allowed to assist terminally ill patients in ending their lives. Thirty-one percent disagree.

Those in the Northeast (73 percent), Catholics (70 percent), white Americans (73 percent), those with graduate degrees (77 percent), Nones (88 percent) and those who skip religious services (78 percent) are among those most likely to agree.

More than half of Southerners (64 percent), African-Americans (53 percent), Protestants (53 percent), those with a high school diploma or less (64 percent) and those who attend services at least once a month (52 percent) also agree.

Again, those with evangelical beliefs (42 percent) do not.

LifeWay Research's findings echo those of other studies. A 2015 Gallup survey found 68 percent of Americans said physician-assisted suicide should be legal, up from 53 percent in 2013. Gallup also found that support for legalized physician-assisted suicide has wavered over the past 20 years. It previously peaked at 68 percent in 2001 before declining to 53 percent.

The debate over physician-assisted suicide is unlikely to go away, says McConnell, and it raises troublesome questions.

"Such requests are asking doctors to betray one of their most sacred oaths—which admits, 'It may also be within my power to take a life,' but concludes, 'I must not play at God,'" says McConnell. "To ask physicians to turn from their task of healing is not a decision to make lightly."

EVALUATING THE AUTHOR'S ARGUMENTS:

In this viewpoint Bob Smietana notes that the majority of Americans favor legal physician-assisted death. Does this mean the country should make physician-assisted death legal everywhere? Why or why not?

Viewpoint 4

Doctors Don't Want Legal Physician-Assisted Suicide

Billy Hallowell

"We oppose active intervention with the intent to produce death for the relief of pain, suffering, or economic considerations, or for the convenience of patient, family, or society."

In the following viewpoint, Billy Hallowell looks at the response of Christian medical professionals to the movement to legalize physician-assisted death. Some medical professionals do not believe that it is ethical to cause death under any conditions. They may refuse to even discuss physician-assisted death as an option when it is legal. In 2016, the Christian Medical and Dental Associations sued the Vermont Board of Medical Practice in federal court. A Vermont law requires physicians to either inform patients about end-of-life care or refer them to a doctor who will. The lawsuit alleges that this forces physicians to violate their conscience and professional ethics. (In 2017, a federal judge dismissed the lawsuit.) Billy Hallowell is a journalist who reports on faith and culture.

"Why So Many Doctors Oppose Euthanasia and Assisted Suicide," by Billy Hallowell, Deseret News, August 4, 2016. Reprinted by permission.

AS YOU READ, CONSIDER THE FOLLOWING QUESTIONS:

1. Why do the Christian Medical and Dental Associations oppose legal physician-assisted death?
2. What does the Vermont law require physicians to do?
3. What is the position of the American Medical Association (AMA) when it comes to physician-assisted death?

As states across the nation consider proposals to legalize doctor-assisted suicide, a longstanding but little known group of Christian medical professionals is doubling down in its opposition by taking proponents of the practice to court.

The Christian Medical and Dental Associations sued the Vermont Board of Medical Practice in federal court on July 19, alleging that physicians are being forced to violate their conscience and professional ethics through a government requirement that they either inform patients about end-of-life care or refer them to a doctor who will.

Dr. David Stevens, CEO of The Christian Medical & Dental Associations, recently told the Deseret News that his organization believes that doctor-assisted suicide is immoral as well as "dangerous for doctors, patients and family."

"As a Christian organization, it's contrary to the Bible. Given life is sacred, we're made in God's image," Stevens said. "All the major religious traditions oppose it."

But beyond the moral implications, he believes that assisted suicide constitutes professional malfeasance, as the "foundation of the doctor-patient relationship is trust."

He questions how someone can fully trust a doctor who has the power to both cure and kill.

Inside the Debate

His comments come as the doctor-assisted suicide debate has ramped up in recent years, specifically after the death of Brittany Maynard, a 29-year-old, cancer-stricken woman who spent the final months of her life imploring the nation to embrace what she and other activists call "death with dignity."

After learning that she had terminal brain cancer, Maynard became an advocate for Compassion & Choices, a group that works to "protect and expand end-of-life options—and to ensure health care providers honor and enable patients' decisions about their care."

She appeared in interviews and commercials throughout 2014 to discuss her terminal diagnosis, and to openly advocate for physician-assisted suicide.

Her battle, including details about how she and her husband moved from California to Oregon, where physician-assisted suicide is legal, sparked heated debate about the moral implications of doctor involvement in the process.

It was in Oregon that Maynard eventually decided to take lethal drugs that were legally prescribed by a doctor. Just weeks before her November 2014 death, she told The Associated Press that her family no longer wished to see her in pain.

"I wanted a cure for my cancer. I still want a cure for my cancer. One does not exist, at least that I'm aware of," Maynard said. "When we all sat down and looked at the facts, there isn't a single person that loves me that wishes me more pain and more suffering."

California has since legalized doctor-assisted suicide; it is also legal in Vermont, Washington and Montana.

Maynard's decision to end her life brought to light an issue that, like many others, has profoundly changed in the eyes of the American public over time.

In 2016, Gallup found that 69 percent of Americans believe that doctors should be able to end the lives of terminal patients using painless means, compared to just 36 percent who believed that in 1950. Over the past decade, acceptance among Americans has ranged from 64 to 75 percent.

But the Christian Medical and Dental Associations are working fervently to turn back the tide of support for doctor-assisted suicide before more states legalize it.

The Associations' History

The Christian Medical and Dental Associations has a long history, with Stevens quipping that the organization is "older than Penicillin."

In general, the number of regular churchgoers that accept or support physician-assisted death has not increased.

Its foundations were set in 1931 when a medical student at Northwest Medical School noticed a Bible on a fellow pupil's desk. That sparked a discussion as well as the idea for the group's creation—and from there it blossomed.

"It began to spread on that campus and then to other campuses," Stevens explained. "We began to see a large movement into missions of Christian doctors across the country."

As it expanded in its size and scope, the organization started working in short-term missions in the 1960s, with its leaders starting to take official stances on public health issues a decade later.

"We really started having ethical positions in the '70s after *Roe v. Wade*," he said, referencing the Supreme Court's landmark abortion decision. "We have over 50 ethical positions on our website."

These positions, which are not binding on membership, outline ethical viewpoints on a plethora of issues, including doctor-assisted suicide.

"We, as Christian physicians and dentists, believe that human life is a gift from God and is sacred because it bears God's image," reads the statement on assisted suicide. "Human life has worth because

Christ died to redeem it, and it has meaning because God has an eternal purpose for it."

It continues, "We oppose active intervention with the intent to produce death for the relief of pain, suffering, or economic considerations, or for the convenience of patient, family, or society."

The organization first approved the language in 1992. It was around that time that the Christian Medical & Dental Associations also started diving a bit deeper into public policy.

The organization today has four main operational functions: working with students, medical missions, training doctors to do media and offering the public information about a litany of health issues.

"We're on 270 plus campuses, where we have CMDA chapters really helping students to integrate their faith into the practice of medicine," Stevens said, noting that there are around 16,000 active members. "We have 800 members who are career missionaries around the world."

Legal Claims

On the assisted suicide front, the Christian Medical & Dental Associations is now asking the courts to uphold conscience protections for doctors and other medical professionals.

The lawsuit filed against Vermont regulators in U.S. District Court in Vermont alleges that health care professionals are being forced to violate their oath "to do no harm."

"According to the agency, only physicians must refer patients to others who will counsel for assisted suicide," reads a statement from conservative legal firm Alliance Defending Freedom. "However, all of the health care professionals filing suit contend it is unethical for them to counsel for, refer for, or in any other way participate in suicide at the hands of medical personnel."

Bridget Asay, solicitor general at the Vermont Attorney General's Office, told the Deseret News that the government plans to defend itself against the complaint, but declined to offer additional details on the matter.

Kevin Diaz, national director of legal advocacy for Compassion & Choices, though, said that his organization is considering filing a friend-of-the-court brief in support of the Vermont Board of Medical Practice.

"The federal judge should dismiss this case, because physicians should not impose their personal values on their patients by preventing them from receiving information about all of their end-of-life care options," Diaz said. "All terminally ill Vermonters should be able to make fully informed decisions about their end-of-life care that are consistent with their own values and faith, and most important, for them and for their families."

Fast Fact

The AMA website lists Code of Medical Ethics opinions both for and against physician-assisted suicide. The opposition opinion states, "Physician-assisted suicide is fundamentally incompatible with the physician's role as healer."

He said that Compassion and Choices believes that a doctor who is unwilling to inform a patient about end-of-life care should "make a referral or otherwise arrange for the patient to receive all relevant information."

Other Concerns

In addition to worries about upholding doctors' conscience rights, one of Stevens' primary concerns is that a widespread acceptance of doctor-assisted suicide could one day morph into a broader embrace of euthanasia.

For many, the two are conflated or synonymous, though Stevens cautioned against that notion. When it comes to physician-assisted suicide, doctors provide patients with information, or give a prescription for fatal sleeping pills.

Euthanasia, however, involves deeper involvement from doctors, and is defined as a situation in which "a lethal agent (is given) by another person to a patient for the purpose of relieving the patient's intolerable and incurable suffering," according to the American Medical Association.

"It takes no great skill for a doctor to kill a patient," Stevens said. "What takes consummate skill is good end-of-life care."

The Christian Medical and Dental Associations is not alone in its opposition to assisted suicide and euthanasia either, as the American

Medical Association—the nation's premiere medical association—also recently affirmed its opposition.

A recently published ethics document details the association's ethical stance. While it proclaims that it is understandable why terminal patients in extreme discomfort might seek death over continued life, the AMA believes that "permitting physicians to engage in assisted suicide would ultimately cause more harm than good."

The text continues, "Physician-assisted suicide is fundamentally incompatible with the physician's role as healer, would be difficult or impossible to control, and would pose serious societal risks."

Stevens said that there are other concerns as well, including whether physician-assisted suicide would encourage the medical system to more regularly put an end to "burdensome patients," especially considering the high cost of health care.

"This whole premise is based on that there is a right not to suffer and an obligation to help people not to suffer," he said. "But how do you measure suffering? Suffering it totally subjective."

This argument becomes particularly pertinent when considering that mental illness has become a benchmark through which people in Belgium have been able to willingly end their lives; psychological disorders are covered under the assisted suicide law there.

It is that dynamic that has Stevens worried about what's to come in the U.S.

"Suicide's not illegal. We're not talking about giving people the right to die," Stevens said. "They can die now if they want to … suicide's not illegal (though) I don't advise it."

He continued, "What you're asking is to wrap the respectability of the medical profession around something that has been a thorn in society."

EVALUATING THE AUTHOR'S ARGUMENTS:

In this viewpoint, Billy Hallowell notes that some doctors refuse to discuss end-of-life options with patients. They may also refuse to refer patients to doctors who will have that discussion. Do doctors have a right to follow their own moral views when it comes to what they discuss with patients? Or do they have an obligation to inform patients of all options? Why?

Viewpoint 5

Doctors Should Help People Die with Dignity

"We have a right to die with dignity, and the medical profession has a duty to assist in that regard."

Anton van Niekerk

In the following viewpoint, Anton van Niekerk writes that in a democracy, people have the right to commit suicide. It may not always be morally correct to execute that right. Yet in the case of terminally ill patients, he believes suicide may be a moral decision. He notes that medical science has allowed people to live longer, but this sometimes comes with suffering and a loss of dignity. In van Niekerk's view, people should be allowed to end their lives in order to avoid this. Anton Albert van Niekerk is professor of philosophy and the director of the Centre for Applied Ethics at Stellenbosch University in South Africa.

AS YOU READ, CONSIDER THE FOLLOWING QUESTIONS:

1. How could legal euthanasia lead to the abuse of vulnerable members of society?
2. Why does the author believe that suicide should be legal in a democracy?
3. How can medicine that prolongs life lead to negative consequences?

"We Have a Right to Die with Dignity. The Medical Profession Has a Duty to Assist," by Anton van Niekerk, The Conversation, October 26, 2016. https://theconversation.com/we-have-a-right-to-die-with-dignity-the-medical-profession-has-a-duty-to-assist-67574.

Euthanasia represents one of the oldest issues in medical ethics. It is forbidden in the original Hippocratic Oath, and has consistently been opposed by most religious traditions since antiquity—other than, incidentally, abortion, which has only been formally banned by the Catholic Church since the middle of the 19th century.

Euthanasia is a wide topic with many dimensions. I will limit myself in this article to the issue of assisted death, which seems to me to be one of the most pressing issues of our time.

Desmond Tutu, emeritus archbishop of Cape Town, raised it again on his 85th birthday in an article in the Washington Post. He wrote:

> *I have prepared for my death and have made it clear that I do not wish to be kept alive at all costs. I hope I am treated with compassion and allowed to pass onto the next phase of life's journey in the manner of my choice.*

Assisted death can take the form of physician assisted suicide (PAS). Here a suffering and terminal patient is assisted by a physician to gain access to a lethal substance which the patient himself or herself takes or administers. If incapable of doing so, the physician—on request of the patient—administers the lethal substance which terminates the patient's life.

The latter procedure is also referred to as "voluntary active euthanasia" (VAE). I will not deal with the issue of involuntary euthanasia –where the suffering patient's life is terminated without their explicit consent—a procedure which, to my mind, is ethically much more problematic.

Passive Form of Euthanasia

The term "voluntary active euthanasia" suggests that there also is a passive form of euthanasia. It is passive in the sense that nothing is "actively" done to kill the patient, but that nothing is done to deter the process of dying either and that the termination of life-support which is clearly futile, is permitted.

However, the moral significance of the distinction between "active" and "passive" euthanasia is increasingly questioned by ethicists. The reason simply is the credibility of arguing that administering a lethal agent is "active," but terminating life support (for example switching off a ventilator) is "passive." Both clearly are observable and describable actions, and both are the direct causes of the patient's death.

There are a number of reasons for the opposition to physician assisted suicide or voluntary active euthanasia. The value bestowed on human life in all religious traditions and almost all cultures, such as the prohibition on murder is so pervasive that it is an element of common, and not statutory, law.

Objections from the medical profession to being seen or utilised as "killers" rather than saviours of human life, as well as the sometimes well-founded fear of the possible abuse of physician assisted suicide or voluntary active euthanasia, is a further reason. The main victims of such possible abuse could well be the most vulnerable and indigent members of society: the poor, the disabled and the like. Those who cannot pay for prolonged accommodation in expensive health care facilities and intensive care units.

Death with Dignity

In support of physician assisted suicide or voluntary active euthanasia, the argument is often made that, as people have the right to live with dignity, they also have the right to die with dignity. Some medical conditions are simply so painful and unnecessarily prolonged that the capability of the medical profession to alleviate suffering by means of palliative care is surpassed.

Intractable terminal suffering robs the victims of most of their dignity. In addition, medical science and practice is currently capable of an unprecedented prolongation of human life. It can be a prolongation that too often results in a concomitant prolongation of unnecessary and pointless suffering.

Enormous pressure is placed upon both families and the health care system to spend time and very costly resources on patients that have little or no chance of recovery and are irrevocably destined to die. It is, so the argument goes, not inhumane or irreverent to assist such patients—particularly if they clearly and repeatedly so request—to bring their lives to an end.

I am personally much more in favour of the pro-PAS and pro-VAE positions, although the arguments against do raise issues that

Should people have the right to die with dignity? Is suicide a right in a democracy, as the author argues?

need to be addressed. Most of those issues (for example the danger of the exploitation of vulnerable patients) I believe, can be satisfactorily dealt with by regulation.

Argument in Favour of Assisted Suicide

The most compelling argument in favour of physician assisted suicide or voluntary active euthanasia is the argument in support of committing suicide in a democracy. The right to commit suicide is, as far as I am concerned, simply one of the prices we have to be willing to pay as citizens of a democracy.

We do not have the right, and we play no discernible role, in coming into existence. But we do have the right to decide how long we remain in existence. The fact that we have the right to suicide, does not mean that it is always (morally) right to execute that right.

It is hard to deny the right of an 85-year-old with terminal cancer of the pancreas and almost no family and friends left, to commit suicide or ask for assisted death. In this case, he or she both has the right, and will be in the right if exercising that right.

Compare that with the situation of a 40-year-old man, a husband and father of three young children, who has embezzled company funds and now has to face the music in court. He, also, has the right to commit suicide. But, I would argue, it would not be morally right for him to do so, given the dire consequences for his family. To have a right, does not imply that it is always right to execute that right.

My argument in favour of physician assisted suicide or voluntary active euthanasia is thus grounded in the right to suicide, which I think is fundamental to a democracy.

Take the case of a competent person who is terminally ill, who will die within the next six months and has no prospect of relief or cure. This person suffers intolerably and/or intractably, often because of

FAST FACT

Doctor-assisted death is sometimes separated into active or passive forms. In the active form, the patient is given something to hurry death. In the passive form, treatments that prolong life are withheld.

an irreversible dependence on life-support. This patient repeatedly, say at least twice a week, requests that his/her life be terminated. I am convinced that to perform physician assisted suicide or voluntary active euthanasia in this situation is not only the humane and respectful, but the morally justified way to go.

The primary task of the medical profession is not to prolong life or to promote health, but to relieve suffering. We have a right to die with dignity, and the medical profession has a duty to assist in that regard.

EVALUATING THE AUTHOR'S ARGUMENTS:

In this viewpoint, author Anton van Niekerk argues that there are times when it is morally acceptable to commit suicide and times when it is not. Do you agree? Why or why not? Should suffering be considered? Should the amount of time someone might have left to live be considered?

Chapter 2

Is Legal Physician-Assisted Suicide Necessary or Useful?

Is physician-assisted death the best solution for chronic pain and suffering?

Viewpoint 1

Palliative Care Is Better Than Assisted Suicide

Liz O'Connor

"We have the technology today to completely eliminate suffering."

In the following viewpoint, Liz O'Connor discusses an alternative to physician-assisted death. She quotes experts who explain the benefits of palliative care. This process focuses on treating suffering rather than ending suffering through a quicker death. The author wrote this report for Catholic News Service. The viewpoint focuses particularly on the response of Catholics to questions about the end of life. The sources quoted suggest that people can learn from the process of dying, and even find benefits in it. Liz O'Connor is an award-winning journalist with a focus on religion and Catholicism.

AS YOU READ, CONSIDER THE FOLLOWING QUESTIONS:

1. What does palliative care attempt to do, according to the viewpoint?
2. How common is access to palliative care?
3. According to the author, how does pain control affect a patient's lifespan?

The much-publicized, physician-assisted suicide in Oregon of 29-year-old Brittany Maynard has reignited discussion of a life-affirming alternative—palliative care.

Palliative care is "the comprehensive management of symptoms and attention to the whole-person needs of a patient with chronic illness especially in its terminal stages," according to Dr. Daniel Sulmasy, professor of medical ethics in the medical and divinity schools at the University of Chicago.

He said it includes pain control, treatment of depression and nausea, fatigue and weakness, among other symptoms, and he noted that most teams also include chaplains to provide spiritual care.

M.C. Sullivan, ethics director of Covenant Health Systems with offices in Tewksbury, Massachusetts, who chairs the board of the Oregon-based Supportive Care Coalition, said too many people don't know about palliative care, and that there's not "good permeation" even in health care organizations. Many have only heard about palliation in the context of end-of-life care, she said, and therefore either fear it or disapprove of it.

With new pain medications and pain technologies, Sullivan said, pain can be controlled or eliminated.

But she said sometimes there has to be a trade-off, and some patients will choose to live with some pain to remain alert and able to interact with loved ones or will be troubled by some side effects of pain medication, such as nausea. Nevertheless, available pain control measures "can reduce even the most severe pain."

Palliative care helps the patient have control. Individuals respond differently and make different choices. Not all hospitals have palliative care teams or palliative care specialists—a 2011 Pew study showed only 30 percent of hospitals having such penetration. But the goal, Sullivan said, is to have informed patient consumers who expect and demand good palliative care: "Then they will get it."

They need to know that most hospitals are now being required to offer palliative care and "they need to feel empowered and to ask (about it) at a time earlier on—as soon as they're diagnosed with serious or chronic illness." There should be, she told Catholic News Service, a "robust" ongoing conversation between patient and caregivers about the patient's current conditions and goals.

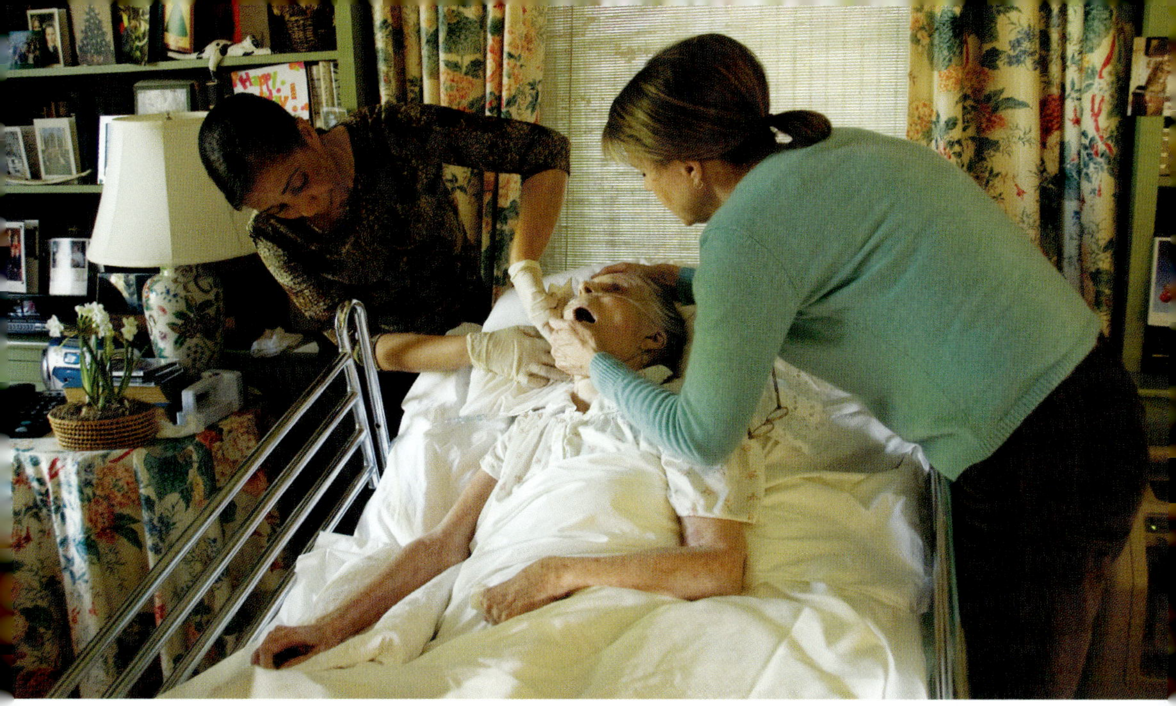

Many terminal patients choose palliative care, which focuses on providing comfort and reducing suffering during the last stage of life.

Palliative care and treatment of disease, including such measures as chemotherapy for cancer, can be used together as appropriate.

Sulmasy also pointed out that the Catholic Church has been teaching for some 500 years that the patient need not accept extraordinary means such as artificial life support when they are burdensome or useless.

Unfortunately, he said, there are "pockets of physicians" who believe in the use of such measures until the very end of a patient's life, and some families who will insist on them when patients cannot express their own preferences.

He said that the things people fear most when they are asking for assisted suicide are being a burden on others or not being in control. They also fear being in intractable pain and being abandoned and alone. Palliative care is "the kind of treatment we can give for the kinds of symptoms people fear."

Dr. Michael Brescia is executive medical director of Calvary Hospital in the Bronx, New York, a hospital devoted exclusively to the care of patients in the end stages of cancer.

He said that he has never had a patient who has spent 24 hours at Calvary ask for assisted suicide. "We're not afraid to use powerful

Fast Fact

The "dying with dignity" movement involves offering options to terminally ill patients, including physician-assisted death, suicide, refusing medical treatments, and refusing food and drink.

drugs to relieve the pain; pain is not an issue."

Maynard had reportedly been told that her brain cancer would cause her to die in terrible pain and to have seizures. If she had had appropriate palliative care, she "would never have been in pain, would never have had seizures, would never have been alone," said Brescia.

While Calvary's philosophy does not include using extraordinary measures to prolong death, he said, speaking of physician-assisted suicide, that "the answer is not to kill (patients) and not to help to kill them," but to treat the suffering.

Maynard's death didn't need to be the way it was, he said; had she come to a place like Calvary, "she would have been a gift to us."

Dr. William Toffler of Portland, Oregon, national director of the Physicians for Compassionate Care Education Foundation, spoke of the euphemisms with which advocates of assisted suicide cloak their agenda. Such terms as "death with dignity" or "compassion in dying" are loaded, he said. "What does this say to the disabled? That they have no dignity?"

Dignity, he said, is inherent in being a human person, and all "have to have the courage" to face the challenges that come with growing older.

His wife of 40 years, he said, died a few months ago after spending her last five years with cancer.

"I get sad every day," Toffler said, but grieving is a part of the human condition. She needed his help at the end of her life, but that didn't mean she died without dignity. During those five years of her illness, he said, "we celebrated her life."

"The idea of killing one another is anathema to our human condition and certainly to our Catholic tradition," he said. When it comes to treatments at the end of life, "we believe in choice" and do not require the use of treatments that may not be helpful or may even be harmful, "but there's a bright line" between declining those treatments and actively hastening death, he said. The latter "is not care, it's killing."

Adequate pain control, Toffler said, tends not to shorten but to extend life. For example, he said morphine is God's gift to the dying and with appropriate dosing "is a tremendously safe drug, incredibly useful and incredibly safe," and can help a patient "to live life well without artificially hastening death." But that means, he said, titrating dosages carefully—perhaps increasing a dose, when needed, by 50 percent, not by 500 percent.

Palliative care, he said, is the perfect answer to advocates of physician assisted suicide. "We have the technology today to completely eliminate suffering," he said, while the promoters of assisted suicide "believe that the solution to suffering is to kill the sufferers."

In Oregon, one of the three states where voters approved making physician-assisted suicide legal, he said some patients have become distrustful of doctors. "It's not part of my profession to coach people in how to kill themselves," but there are doctors who do that. He said he has had patients ask him, "Is that doctor one of those death doctors?" The mentality among some doctors has become "if it's a difficult problem you just help the person kill himself or herself."

"Death can be beautiful, but it's never pretty," Sulmasy said.

Nevertheless, the medical and nursing professions can promise effective treatments, and the dying need to know "that they really have something to teach us," something that should be cherished and valued by the rest of us, he said.

Patients too often don't see what are offered to them as opportunities for growth, the ability to live a full human life even in their final days, he added.

EVALUATING THE AUTHOR'S ARGUMENTS:

In this viewpoint, Liz O'Connor cites sources that argue that physician-assisted death is not necessary. Instead, they claim, palliative care can address suffering so people are willing to die naturally. Do you think palliative care could always be an alternative to physician-assisted death? Why or why not?

Viewpoint 2

Palliative Care and Assisted Dying Can Work Together

David Clark

"Most values of palliative care workers and advocates of euthanasia are shared."

In the following viewpoint, David Clark further compares physician-assisted death and palliative care. He notes that people often have strong opinions in favor of one or the other. Those who favor palliative care insist it is a better alternative to physician-assisted death. Yet few countries have successfully offered palliative care to everyone. In addition, evidence shows that palliative care and physician-assisted death can coexist. As an example, the country of Belgium ranks high for both palliative care and euthanasia. This may suggest, the author notes, that even when people have good palliative care, some will choose to end their lives more quickly. David Clark is a professor of medical sociology at the University of Glasgow in Scotland.

"Palliative Care or Assisted Dying? We Just Need to Start Talking More About 'The Right to Die Well,'" by David Clark, The Conversation, March 30, 2016. https://theconversation.com/palliative-care-or-assisted-dying-we-just-need-to-start-talking-more-about-the-right-to-die-well-56258.

AS YOU READ, CONSIDER THE FOLLOWING QUESTIONS:

1. How many countries have successfully included palliative care in their health services?
2. In the United States, has the focus been more on improving palliative care or legalizing physician-assisted death?
3. Is there evidence that legalized physician-assisted death leads to less palliative care?

In most parts of the world the proponents of palliative care and of assisted dying do not see eye to eye. Palliative care activists say the problems that lead to assisted dying requests can usually be dealt with in ways that do not hasten death. They promote quality of life and reject the idea of "dying on demand". Supporters of assisted dying, on the other hand, argue that palliative care cannot be effective in every case. To them, the important thing is to respect autonomy and freedom of choice.

It's unclear whether these two approaches can be reconciled.

Relations between supporters of palliative care and of assisted dying have a history of tension, even antagonism. Dame Cicely Saunders, founder of the modern hospice movement, was fond of going head-to-head in debates with members of the Voluntary Euthanasia Society in the 1960s, for example. More recently, the society's change of name to Dignity in Dying in 2006 antagonised the hospice and palliative care world by implying that its practitioners did not have the monopoly on a dignified end.

Just last year, a group of experts representing the European Association for Palliative Care again declared that the provision of euthanasia and assisted dying should not be included in the practice of palliative care—a position that has remained unchanged for the last two decades.

The British Medical Association likewise remains opposed to the legalisation of assisted dying in any form, though in a series of recent reports it said it now seeks "to move debate beyond oversimplistic for/against positioning to consider some of the complex issues surrounding physician-assisted dying, its potential complexities and changing legislative and practical frameworks".

Over the years, however, palliative care has struggled to gain traction. Indeed, my own research has shown that just 20 countries in the world have achieved "advanced integration" of their palliative care services with the wider health and social care system.

The UK is ranked the best place to die when it comes to palliative care, according to an index constructed by the Economist Intelligence Unit (EIU). But there have been obvious failings and shortcomings in the delivery of palliative care at scale. We see these in the furore over the Liverpool Care Pathway and in poor reports on end of life care from the ombusdman and the Care Quality Commission.

FAST FACT

Several universities and research groups conduct end of life studies. They attempt to address challenges in end-of-life care and explore how people choose to die, the meanings we attach to dying, and the rituals associated with dying, among other topics.

Would legalised assisted dying have any bearing on these problems? We only have a few examples to go on.

Legalising Assisted Death

Euthanasia and/or physician assisted dying are currently legal in just four countries: the Netherlands (2001), Belgium (2002) and Luxembourg (2009) have all legalised euthanasia. This means it is legal in these countries, provided certain procedures and protocols are followed, for a doctor to kill a patient at their informed and competent request.

In the US, individual states have focused their efforts on the legalisation of physician assisted suicide, though the broader term "aid in dying" is now being adopted by some. This involves a doctor in a process to prescribe lethal drugs to a person who, following defined procedures, has resolved to end their own life by taking the drugs, and then does so. It was legalised in Oregon in 1997 and more recently was taken up by Washington State, Montana, and Vermont. California will soon follow when its End of Life Option Act comes into effect on June 9.

Elderly and seriously ill patients may consider speaking with their physician about adopting an end-of-life care strategy.

By long standing arrangement, Switzerland does not prosecute those who assist a suicide, provided they do not benefit from the outcome.

In locations where either physician assisted suicide or euthanasia are legalised, there is no evidence this inhibits the development of palliative care. In Oregon, most of the very small numbers of people who avail themselves of the Death with Dignity Act are actually on hospice programmes. In the Netherlands, palliative care services, research and education appear to have thrived in the period since euthanasia was fully legalised, though they were underdeveloped before that.

Belgium provides the most interesting example: it has almost 200 palliative care services, is in the list of 20 countries with "advanced integration" of palliative care and was ranked fifth worldwide in the EIU's "quality of death" index. It is also home to academic research groups studying end of life issues as well as leading professors in the field—yet in Belgium about one death in 20 results from euthanasia.

The Flanders Model

Something unique has happened in the Flanders region of Belgium: the practice of euthanasia and the delivery of palliative care have been brought together in a single "integral" model. Here no contradiction is seen delivering the best pain and symptom management and the holistic psycho-social support that palliative care has to offer, while also enabling a person's life to be ended at their request, by a physician.

The Flanders model offends some and inspires others. But, as the authors of one of the few studies on the matter conclude:

> *Most values of palliative care workers and advocates of euthanasia are shared. If Belgium's experience applies elsewhere, advocates of the legalisation of euthanasia have every reason to promote palliative care, and activists for palliative care need not oppose the legalisation of euthanasia.*

Should assisted dying and the delivery of palliative care exist side by side? Their shared aim would be to provide relief from suffering, support dignity and also allow the freedom to determine the manner and timing of one's own death. Flanders and Oregon hint that this approach can work, and we intend to look at this further in our Wellcome Trust-funded study on Global Interventions at the End of Life.

It is perhaps time to bring down the ethical and ideological wire fence which has for so long separated the two approaches to the end of life: palliative care and assisted dying. Once this barrier has been removed we might more fully explore how best to deliver dignity and choice to the growing number of people who will die in the world every year.

EVALUATING THE AUTHOR'S ARGUMENTS:

In this viewpoint, author David Clark notes that Belgium has high ranks of both palliative care and euthanasia. What can we learn from this? What more might you want to know before determining if one option is better than the other?

Viewpoint 3

The Mentally Ill Have a Right to End Their Lives

"Asking his tormented soul to stay here and suffer seemed cruel, when death might provide relief."

Kelly Burch

In the following viewpoint, Kelly Burch asks whether suicide is a reasonable choice for people with mental illnesses. The author relays a personal story of how she watched her own father struggle with mental illness as treatments failed him. At first she felt guilty about even considering suicide as an option for him. Over time, she recognized that his suffering might be unbearable. Burch argues that family members and medical professionals often think a person can get better if they simply try harder. Mental illness is more complicated than that. Despite the fact that her father did improve, the author says she would not have blamed him for choosing suicide. Kelly Burch is a freelance writer who shares stories of family and mental health.

"The Mentally Ill Should Be Allowed to End Their Lives," by Kelly Burch, Medium.com, February 15, 2017. Reprinted by permission.

AS YOU READ, CONSIDER THE FOLLOWING QUESTIONS:

1. What attitudes do societies have about living a long life?
2. How is mental illness different from terminal illnesses usually associated with physician-assisted death?
3. Why do people with mental illnesses tend to die sooner than others, even without considering suicide?

I was out to lunch when I first realized that suicide was a rational choice for my father. He was once again in the psych ward for depression, and I was trying to piece myself back together after visiting him. At that point, he was about three years into a ten-year depression that would render him unable to work, live on his own, or even get out of bed some days. Three years may not seem like very long, but watching my father suffer day after day as each new treatment failed was incredibly painful for our family. To live it, I realized, it must be unbearable.

"It's not fair to expect him to stay," I thought to myself. Although I don't have any strong religious convictions, asking his tormented soul to stay here and suffer seemed cruel, when death might provide relief. Yet just allowing myself to internally acknowledge that suicide may be an option seemed dangerous and taboo. It would be years until I mentioned the thought to anyone, and even then I whispered it quietly, shyly, in a support group for family members of people with mental illness. When I saw everyone in the room slowly nodding in agreement, I was both relieved and heartbroken.

American society, as with many cultures around the globe, values longevity of life. We despise premature death. In fact, after a cursory internet scan, I've been unable to find any societies that don't value long lives, with the exception of dying on the battlefield.

"One of the oldest human drives is to want to stay alive as long as possible," said Jessica Nutik Zitter, a doctor who has written about end of life issues. "I think we are still of the belief that the more time we have, the better."

It's often presumed that a long life is accompanied with more happiness and joy. But I fear we might be projecting this belief onto

Should people who suffer with severe mental illness be allowed to end their lives? How does this differ from physician-assisted death for elderly or terminally ill patients?

people with longterm mental illness and addiction, for whom each day can bring unimaginable suffering.

Americans are willing to allow death as a means to end physical pain. In 2016, 69 percent of Americans believed that euthanasia should be legal when the person has a disease that cannot be cured, and nearly half said that they would consider ending their own lives if faced with a terminal illness. But what if the condition isn't technically terminal? What if it is an invisible illness that will lead to years of suffering in an internal, sometimes inescapable, hell?

Last year, news broke about Mark Langedijk, a 41-year-old alcoholic in the Netherlands who chose to end his life through legal euthanasia. In the Netherlands, mental illness is a factor in about 1 percent of euthanasia cases, up tenfold from 2010. People around the globe expressed outrage about Langedijk's death, but his brother shared the family's story openly in order to spark conversations about mental illness.

"You can close your eyes to it and keep telling yourself everyone is curable but the fact remains, not everyone is," Marcel Langedijk told The Independent. "Alcoholism and depression are illnesses, just like cancer. People who suffer from it need a humane way out."

However, society continues to place value judgments on people with addiction and mental illness, convinced that they could improve if only they tried a little harder.

"I think there is a lot of unconscious resistance amongst psychiatrists against the idea of euthanasia," said Dutch psychiatrist Paulan Stärcke, who last year gave a speech entitled, "Condemned to live with unbearable psychiatric suffering, or allowed to die?" Resistance to euthanasia for the mentally ill is just one of the ways that our society disenfranchises this population by speaking at them about what they "should" do, rather than listening to their lived experiences.

"The people around people with mental illness think they know better," my dad told me. "With family and friends and caregivers there is a mistrust that the person with mental illness can take care of themselves."

This mistrust doesn't just factor into the big issues, like whether to live or die. It also affects how we view people with severe mental illness in everyday interactions.

Last year, I reported on the fact that people with mental illness die 25 years younger than their peers, often from preventable physical diseases like hypertension and diabetes. There are programs that aim to close the life expectancy gap, which focus on behaviors like smoking cessation, healthy eating, and exercise. Those are all wonderful in theory—but too often, cigarettes and food provide just a little bit of comfort to people who are struggling with mental illness each day.

Despite being diabetic and having had a stroke, my father drinks Coca-Cola more than water and smokes like a chimney. This used to make me rage, until I realized that these habits provide his only physical and mental comfort in his turbulent daily existence. Who am I to ask him to give that up?

Yes, in an ideal world, people would have healthier coping mechanisms. However, I'm uncomfortable with people who

Fast Fact

According to the Centers for Disease Control and Prevention, more than 50 percent of people will be diagnosed with a mental illness or disorder during their lifetime. One in twenty-five Americans live with a serious mental illness.

haven't lived with mental illness telling patients to forfeit a small amount of pleasure in order to prolong a life that is painful to live.

Ken Jue, who founded a program to increase life expectancy for people with mental illness, knows that sometimes advocates with good intentions end up discounting the very people they are trying to help. "That sense of control is so important to people's sense of self integrity," he said. "We lose sight of that in our efforts to help people."

Mine is not the only family to realize that for people with mental illness, a long life is not always better. Although no one would advocate for suicide during a mental health crisis, the handful of my peers that I've discussed this with have admitted that they would accept if their family member rationally chose to end their life, just like Mark Langedijk.

My father is now stable, and thankfully doing well. Sometimes, as in the case of my father, things do get better. While I am grateful to have my dad here, there is no denying that his stabilization came after a decade of hell in the form of time, energy, and money. I would not blame him if he had chosen not to go through that.

EVALUATING THE AUTHOR'S ARGUMENTS:

Viewpoint author Kelly Burch argues that suicide is a reasonable response to mental illness that does not respond to treatment. Do you agree? If so, for how long should someone attempt to get treatment first? Should society support people with mental illnesses in ending their lives, or encourage them to keep trying to get better? How much suffering is enough to warrant an early death? Who gets to decide these questions?

Viewpoint 4

Physician-Assisted Death Harms Society

Ryan Anderson

"The real challenge facing society is to make quality end-of-life care available to all."

In the following viewpoint, Ryan Anderson argues against legalizing physician-assisted death. He says most people simply want to escape suffering. If they can get relief and comfort, they no longer desire suicide. The viewpoint notes that palliative care is not available to everyone, as it should be. The author suggests that medical students need more training in helping people at the end-of-life. He argues that physician-assisted death harms the medical profession. He also says that it encourages society to view elderly people and those with disabilities as burdens. Therefore, physician-assisted death should not be made legal. Ryan Anderson researches and writes about topics involving ethics, religious liberty and political philosophy, and is a research fellow at The Heritage Foundation.

"The Alternative to Physician-Assisted Suicide: Respect Human Dignity and Offer True Compassion," by Ryan Anderson, The Heritage Foundation, May 18, 2015. Reprinted by permission.

AS YOU READ, CONSIDER THE FOLLOWING QUESTIONS:

1. What reasons does this author's group give for opposing physician-assisted death?
2. What reasons did people give for choosing assisted suicide, according to the Oregon study mentioned?
3. How should medical students be trained with regards to palliative care, according to this viewpoint?

Allowing physician-assisted suicide (PAS) would be a grave mistake for four reasons, as explained in a Heritage Foundation Backgrounder, "Always Care, Never Kill."[1] First, it would endanger the weak and vulnerable. Second, it would corrupt the practice of medicine and the doctor–patient relationship. Third, it would compromise the family and intergenerational commitments. And fourth, it would betray human dignity and equality before the law. Instead of helping people to kill themselves, we should offer them appropriate medical care and human presence.

This *Issue Brief* focuses on alternatives to physician-assisted suicide. People seeking PAS typically suffer from depression or other mental illnesses, as well as simply from loneliness. We should respond to suffering with true compassion and solidarity. For those in physical pain, pain management and other palliative medicine can manage their symptoms effectively. For those for whom death is imminent, hospice care and fellowship can accompany them in their last days. Anything less falls short of what human dignity requires. The real challenge facing society is to make quality end-of-life care available to all.

Mental Health and Palliative Care: True Compassionate Treatment

Instead of embracing PAS, we should respond to suffering with true compassion. Most people seeking PAS suffer from depression or other mental illnesses, physical illness, or simply loneliness. Dr. Aaron Kheriaty notes:

> *Suicidal individuals typically do not want to die; they want to escape what they perceive as intolerable suffering. When comfort or relief is offered, in the form of more-adequate treatment for depression, better pain management, or more-comprehensive palliative care, the desire for suicide wanes.*[2]

Rather than helping suicidal people to kill themselves, we should offer them treatment and support. For those in physical pain, palliative care and other pain management can manage their symptoms effectively. For those for whom death is imminent, hospice care and fellowship to accompany them in their last days is what a true death with dignity looks like. Victoria Reggie Kennedy has said it best:

> *My late husband Sen. Edward Kennedy called quality, affordable health care for all the cause of his life. [PAS] turns his vision of health care for all on its head by asking us to endorse patient suicide—not patient care—as our public policy for dealing with pain and the financial burdens of care at the end of life. We're better than that. We should expand palliative care, pain management, nursing care and hospice, not trade the dignity and life of a human being for the bottom line.*[3]

Palliative care focuses on improving a patient's quality of life by alleviating pain and other distressing symptoms of a serious illness. Palliative care is an option for people of any age at any stage in illness, whether that illness is curable, chronic, or life threatening.

When a patient receives a terminal or life-altering diagnosis, the subsequent life changes are not limited to the medical challenges. Patients encounter the physical trauma of the medical diagnosis while also experiencing psychological difficulties, social changes, and even existential concerns. In Oregon Health Authority research, 91 percent of those who were assisted with suicide cited loss of autonomy as their motivation to end their lives, and 71 percent cited loss of dignity as their motivation. Only 31 percent cited inadequate pain control.[4] These needs require different forms of care. Palliative care seeks to take into consideration every facet of the patient's situation—with professionals who can attend to all aspects of the patient's needs.

With hospice and palliative care, patients are able to live their last days at home, surrounded by family and other familiar comforts.

The most common structure in which patients receive palliative care is in hospice. Hospice care can be provided in patients' homes, hospice centers, hospitals, long-term care facilities, or wherever a patient resides. By rejecting PAS and committing to palliative care and hospice care, we can better people's lives at the end of life. As Dr. Leon Kass notes:

> *We must care for the dying, not make them dead. By accepting mortality yet knowing that we will not kill, doctors can focus on enhancing the lives of those who are dying, with relief of pain and discomfort, moral and social support, and, when appropriate, the removal of technical interventions that are merely useless or degrading additions to the burdens of dying.*[5]

Regrettably, palliative care is not as widely available as it should be. The United States has only one palliative care physician for every 1,200 persons living with a serious or life-threatening illness. Even with the aging population, only 63 percent of hospitals report a palliative care program.[6]

In order to increase the availability and understanding of palliative care, medical schools should ensure that students are trained in managing pain and other common distressing symptoms and that they learn how to talk to patients about palliative options at the end of life. As Drs. Hendin and Foley note, when there is a lack of comprehensive support for patients with terminal or life-altering diagnosis, "the focus shifts away from relieving the distress of dying patients considering a hastened death to meeting the statutory requirements for assisted suicide."[7] This we must resist.

FAST FACT

According to the Hospice Foundation of America, hospice is "Medical care to help someone with a terminal illness live as well as possible for as long as possible, increasing quality of life."

Conclusion: Always to Care, Never to Kill

Doctors should help their patients die a dignified natural death, but doctors should not assist in killing or self-killing. Physicians are always to care, never to kill.

Physician-assisted suicide endangers the weak and marginalized in society. Where PAS has been allowed, safeguards that were put in place to minimize this risk have proved inadequate and over time have been weakened or eliminated altogether.

Introducing PAS changes the culture in which medicine is practiced. It corrupts the profession of medicine by permitting the tools of healing to be used as techniques for killing. It also distorts the doctor–patient relationship by reducing patients' trust of doctors and doctors' undivided commitment to the healing of their patients. Physician-assisted suicide also creates perverse incentives for insurance providers and the financing of health care.

Worse yet, PAS negatively affects our entire culture. The temptation to view elderly or disabled family members as burdens will increase, as will the temptation for elderly and disabled family members to view themselves as burdens. Instead of solidarity through civil society and true compassion, PAS creates quick-fix, discriminatory, and lethal solutions.

The most profound injustice of PAS is that it violates human dignity and denies equality before the law. Every human being has intrinsic dignity and is the subject of immeasurable worth. No natural right to PAS exists, and arguments for such a right are incoherent. A legal system that sought to vindicate a right to assisted suicide would jeopardize the real natural right to life for all of its citizens.

For all of these reasons, citizens and policymakers need to resist the push for physician-assisted suicide.[8]

Endnotes

1. See Ryan T. Anderson, "Always Care, Never Kill: How Physician-Assisted Suicide Endangers the Weak, Corrupts Medicine, Compromises the Family, and Violates Human Dignity and Equality," Heritage Foundation Backgrounder No. 3004, March 24, 2015, http://www.heritage.org/research/reports/2015/03/always-care-never-kill-how-physician-assisted-suicide-endangers-the-weak-corrupts-medicine-compromises-the-family-and-violates-human-dignity-and-equality.

2. Aaron Kheriaty, "Apostolate of Death," First Things, April 2015, p. 19.

3. Victoria Reggie Kennedy, "Question 2 Insults Kennedy's Memory," Cape Cod Times, November 3, 2012, http://www.capecodtimes.com/article/20121027/OPINION/210270347 (accessed March 5, 2015).

4. Oregon Public Health Division, "Oregon's Death with Dignity Act—2014."

5. Leon R. Kass, "Dehumanization Triumphant," First Things, August 1996, http://www.firstthings.com/article/1996/08/002-dehumanization-triumphant (accessed January 28, 2015). Elsewhere, Kass adds that "death with dignity, understood as living dignifiedly in the face of death, is not a matter of pulling plugs or taking poison." Leon R. Kass, Life, Liberty and the Defense of Dignity: The Challenge for Bioethics (San Francisco: Encounter Books, 2002), p. 249.

6. R. Sean Morrison and Diane E. Meier, "America's Care of Serious Illness: A State-by-State Report Card on Access to Palliative Care in Our Nation's Hospitals," Center to Advance Palliative Care and the National Palliative Care Research Center, May 2011, p. 9, http://reportcard.capc.org/pdf/state-by-state-report-card.pdf (accessed January 30, 2015).

7. Herbert Hendin and Kathleen Foley, "Physician-Assisted Suicide in Oregon: A Medical Perspective," Michigan Law Review, Vol. 106, No. 8 (June 2008), p. 1616.

8. Anderson, "Always Care, Never Kill."

EVALUATING THE AUTHOR'S ARGUMENTS:

In this viewpoint, author Ryan Anderson argues that assisted suicide harms society. Consider each of the author's points in turn. Do you agree that physician-assisted death harms the medical profession, endangers the weak, negatively affects our culture, and violates human dignity? Why or why not?

Viewpoint 5

People Have Other Ways to Hasten Death

"With accompanying standard palliative care measures, individuals can escape conditions they consider to be worse than death."

Vicki D. Lachman

In the following excerpted viewpoint, Vicki D. Lachman looks at options available to people who wish to hasten their deaths at the end of their lives. One such option is the voluntary stopping of eating and drinking (VSED). VSED can lead to death in a relatively short time, and discomfort can be controlled through medication. The author notes that many nurses are uncomfortable discussing VSED as an option for fear of influencing patients' decisions. However, she writes, many patients are comforted simply knowing they have options for a way out, even if they do not ultimately use them. Vicki D. Lachman is chair of the American Nurses Association Ethics and Human Rights Advisory Board.

AS YOU READ, CONSIDER THE FOLLOWING QUESTIONS:

1. What three conditions are mentioned as the test of informed consent?
2. How soon does death occur after a patient stops eating and drinking?
3. According to the viewpoint, is death by terminal dehydration painful?

"Voluntary Stopping of Eating and Drinking: An Ethical Alternative to Physician-Assisted Suicide," by Vicki D. Lachman, MEDSURG Nursing. Reprinted by permission.

The polarized debate over physician-assisted suicide (PAS) (now sometimes referred to as assisted dying) has included little discussion on an alternative method for voluntary death—terminal dehydration (Miller, Fins, & Snyder, 2000; Miller & Meier, 1998). With terminal dehydration, competent patients with a terminal or incurable illness seek death by forgoing artificial nutrition and hydration or by ceasing to eat or drink. With accompanying standard palliative care measures, individuals can escape conditions they consider to be worse than death. Clinical, ethical, and policy issues will be analyzed primarily by comparing voluntary stopping of eating and drinking (VSED) to PAS. Recommendations for nursing practice, education, and organizational policy will be provided.

Clinicians with palliative care expertise generally agree how to respond to requests for aid in dying (Schwarz, 2014). They begin to explore the reasons behind the request, intensify efforts to relieve pain and suffering, consult specialists for relief of psychological or spiritual suffering, commit to nonabandonment, and seek mutually acceptable solutions for the patient's suffering (Schwarz, 2014). If unacceptable suffering persists despite all efforts, then decisionally capable patients should be informed about all legal options that permit a hastened death (Hospice and Palliative Nurses Association [HPNA], 2011). These options include withholding or VSED, withdrawing life-sustaining interventions, and sedation to unconscious for relief of intractable suffering (HPNA, 2011; Schwarz, 2007).

[…]

Ethical Differences in PAS and VSED

Is PAS—killing oneself by ingesting prescribed lethal medication—primarily dissimilar from refusal of life sustaining treatment or VSED, to which every person has a legal and ethical right? All three of these choices must meet the test of informed consent: patient capacity, voluntariness, and comprehension of the benefit, burden, and consequences (ANA, 2015). Though the outcome in all three is death, nurses have an obligation to inform patients of all options, even PAS if legal in states where they practice.

[…]

Withdrawal of Life-Sustaining Treatment

The courts have stated consistently there is no legal or ethical difference between withholding and withdrawing of life-sustaining interventions. The cases of Karen Quinlan, Nancy Cruzan, and Theresa Schiavo were right-to-die instances that required the withdrawing of life-sustaining treatment (Fine, 2005). In hospitals across this country, clinical decisions to withdraw or withhold treatment occur every day. The informed patient makes a decision not to pursue further treatment or to withdraw treatment already begun (e.g., chemotherapy, left ventricular assist device implantation).

"A valid refusal is sufficient to authorize the withdrawal of treatment, regardless of the clinicians' judgments concerning the medical or moral appropriateness of the action" (Miller et al., 2000, p. 473). Once the valid refusal is made, the physician has a moral responsibility to honor the refusal and/or transfer the patient to another physician. Nurses also may experience discomfort in honoring a patient's autonomous choice to allow death. They can voice conscientious objection when their moral integrity is at risk of being compromised and ask for a replacement in the care of the patient (ANA, 2015; Lachman, 2014).

Voluntary Stopping of Eating and Drinking

Another legal alternative in all 50 states to PAS is VSED; some authors see this simply as a choice of stopping life-sustaining treatment (Lachman, 2010; Miller et al., 2000; Miller & Meier, 1998; Valente, 2004). Food and water are required for life; deciding to forgo these basic elements for continued life support in VSED is done to hasten death. VSED is a volitional refusal, not the natural desire for decreased food and fluids seen in patients in some terminal conditions. When a person stops eating and drinking, death occurs in 1-3

Fast Fact

Palliative sedation, the administration of medicine to put a patient in a state where they have little or no awareness, is legal everywhere in the United States. However, policies about using it vary among different hospitals and hospices.

Rather than taking extraordinary and irreversible measures, some people stop taking food and drink in order to hasten their deaths.

weeks (Valente, 2004). Support by caregivers is needed to manage the dying process, as the patient lapses into unconsciousness.

The arguments for and against VSED involve the conflicting ethical principles of nonmaleficence and autonomy. Persons who argue against the option of VSED (nonmaleficence) frame the actions taken by the individual as suicide and believe it is morally wrong to be complicit in the care of patients who come to this decision (Jansen & Sulmasy, 2002). Lowey (2001) argued a distinction between physicians recommending VSED and patients who come to the decision on their own. Other authors suggested patients have a right to know they can make this choice and should be informed, as they believe only the person living with a terminal illness can know when the burdens outweigh the benefits of continuing to live (Berry, 2009; Miller & Meier, 1998; Schwarz, 2014). The patient's option to voluntarily stop eating and drinking is grounded in the ethical principle of autonomy and is supported by statutory and case law (Miller & Meier, 1998).

Physicians' and nurses' reluctance in discussing VSED as an option often comes from fear of catalyzing an individual's action that will hasten death. However, VSED offers the opportunity for change of mind. Often just knowing a way out exists if the dying process is unbearable can provide relief from desperation that could lead to a more violent solution (Schwarz, 2014). These same phenomena exist in the studies of Oregon patients who actually used a barbiturate to end their lives vs. those who did not use; consistently, approximately half of persons who obtained the barbiturate actually used the lethal dose of medication (Lachman, 2010).

The only research found on refusal of food and fluids involved a survey of 307 nurses and 83 social workers who provided direct care for Oregon residents enrolled in hospice (Harvath et al., 2004). No significant difference was found between nurses and social workers in their support for patients choosing PAS or VSED. More than 75% of participants thought VSED should be an option for patients experiencing physical, psychological, or spiritual suffering; 95.4% would continue to care for patients who choose this option, and 70.7% would consider the option for themselves. Both groups were significantly more supportive of VSED than PAS, with the magnitude of the difference for nurses being larger.

Pope and Anderson (2010) provided an in-depth review of VSED as a legal treatment option at end of life, but their review also offered an excellent comparison to PAS and limiting life-sustaining therapies. They emphasized the importance of educating patients on this choice and honoring appropriate patient requests for VSED. Because of the reluctance of some providers to honor requests for VSED, they suggested, "it may be necessary both to mandate disclosure of VSED as an option and to clarify safe harbor protection for supervising and supporting it" (p. 427).

Managing the Clinical Nursing Issues of Terminal Dehydration

Evidence indicates death by terminal dehydration is not painful when resultant discomfort is managed by palliative care measures (Berry, 2009; Critchlow & Bauer-Wu, 2002; Miller & Meier, 1998). Reduction of fluids reduces urine output, gastrointestinal secretions, pulmonary and pharyngeal secretions, and edema. Critchlow and Bauer-Wu (2002) reported studies in which hospice nurses had a positive view of terminal dehydration, while acute care nurses believed patients needed artificial nutrition and hydration. Experienced nurses who had witnessed the dehydration process had significantly more positive perceptions of terminal dehydration than nurses who had not.

[…]

EVALUATING THE AUTHOR'S ARGUMENTS:

In this viewpoint Vicki D. Lachman notes that even where physician-assisted death is not available, patients have options to hasten the end of their lives. Do you think these options mean that physician-assisted death is not necessary? Why or why not?

Chapter 3

Should Physician-Assisted Suicide Be Legalized?

Several state supreme courts have heard arguments regarding physician-assisted death.

Viewpoint 1

Legal Euthanasia Leads to Abuse

Anita Carey

"It's a lot cheaper to grab a couple drugs and kill you than it is to provide you life-sustaining therapy."

In the following viewpoint, Anita Carey claims that insurance companies encourage assisted suicide. In some cases, insurance companies have suggested a doctor recommend physician-assisted death rather than therapies that would lengthen patients' lives. In one case, the insurance company refused to pay for treatment but offered to pay for end-of-life drugs. Laws that allow for physician-assisted death are supposed to include safeguards that protect patients. The author claims that those safeguards are false or inadequate. She further claims that legal physician-assisted death will lead to a variety of problems, including involuntary euthanasia (without the patient's consent). Anita Carey is a staff writer for Church Militant, a Catholic news website.

AS YOU READ, CONSIDER THE FOLLOWING QUESTIONS:

1. How could an insurance company benefit if patients choose physician-assisted suicide rather than medical treatments?
2. What concerns do people have at the end of life, according to this viewpoint?
3. How could legal physician-assisted death lead to medical systems where pain is not properly managed?

"Insurance Companies Pushing Assisted Suicide to Save Money," by Anita Carey, Church Militant, May 31, 2017. Reprinted by permission.

Insurance companies are choosing profit over protection of life, denying life-saving treatments while pushing clients to opt for assisted suicide instead.

A video released Wednesday by the Patients Rights Action Fund shows Dr. Brian Callister claiming insurance companies pressured him to recommend lethal medication to clients rather than life-saving treatment, in order to save the insurance companies money. He claims his recommended procedures for two different patients with non-fatal conditions were denied coverage, the companies opting to offer cheaper, assisted suicide drug coverage instead.

While speaking with the insurance agents, Callister said that, in two separate incidents, the agents asked if he had considered assisted suicide. Callister says he was "stunned."

"It's a lot cheaper to grab a couple drugs and kill you than it is to provide you life-sustaining therapy," he commented.

Previously, neither Callister nor his patients had discussed assisted suicide. In one case, there was a 70-percent chance for the patient to be cured by the procedure, while the other patient had a 50-percent chance. Both patients "would have been terminal" if they did not have the procedures and both lived in states where assisted suicide was legal.

It's not the only example of the practice. In 2012, Stephanie Packer was diagnosed with scleroderma, a fatal auto-immune disease that attacks a person's internal organs. Packer lives in California, where the Aid-In-Dying law was passed in a special legislative session, without a public vote and signed into law in 2015 by Gov. Jerry Brown, a former Jesuit seminary student.

The insurance company denied coverage for Packer's treatments that would prolong her life. Instead, it offered her lethal drugs with a modest co-pay of only $1.20. Packer, the mother of four young children and a practicing Catholic, refused to kill herself and was left to pay for the medical treatments herself. Eventually, the insurance company began paying for the medical treatments, but not before the family went heavily into debt.

Packer has since become a patient advocate and spokesperson for end-of-life issues, but is still struggling to pay off the debt, leaving her family coping with food shortages and worn-out shoes for her children.

Will insurance companies eventually have the power to decide whether patients should be prescribed life-sustaining treatment or assisted suicide?

Proponents of assisted suicide claim it is a personal choice meant to ease suffering. In a recent talk at the Canadian Catholic Bioethics Institute, Cdl. Gerhard Müller, the Vatican's doctrine chief, refuted these claims, calling them "internally incoherent and fatally flawed."

Cardinal Müller asserted that the claim that suicide does not affect anyone else is a "detachment from the reality of our shared life," noting that "even social science evidence has demonstrated that suicide can be 'contagious.'"

"If the rationale for legal euthanasia is rooted primarily in autonomy, there can be no internally coherent limits on its practice," he said.

Assisted-suicide proponents also claim laws contain safeguards, even "redundent safeguards" such as those claimed by so-called "death expert" Jan Bernheim. In reality, the legislated safeguards are false. A special report by Dr. Laura Dunn and published Wednesday in the *Psychiatric Times* found that in all of the six states that have decriminalized euthanasia:

> *none of the current state statutes specifically mandate a mental health evaluation by a licensed psychiatrist or psychologist prior to the writing of a lethal prescription. Instead, the laws*

place the responsibility for determining the requesting patient's decision-making capacity and mental health status on the "attending physician."

FAST FACT

The worry that legal voluntary euthanasia will lead to involuntary euthanasia is a "slippery slope argument." This type of argument assumes that something relatively harmless may start a trend toward something unthinkable.

In a review of post-death questionaires, Dr. Dunn found the "three most frequently mentioned end-of-life concerns were: decreasing ability to participate in activities that made life enjoyable (96.2 percent), loss of autonomy (92.4 percent), and loss of dignity (75.4 percent)."

Dunn claims these are the mental health issues psychiatrists and psychologists are meant to treat. Müller concurs, saying "the desire for suicide often departs once mental illness and pain are effectively treated. This is true even among the terminally ill."

To refute the position that killing patients eases suffering, the Vatican cardinal mentioned Oregon, the first state to decriminalize euthanasia, as ranking among the lowest in pain management. "This is because once euthanasia is an option, it quickly becomes the path of least resistance for medical decisionmakers," he noted, "leading to an overall decrease in developing and pursuing creative pain management techniques, which in turn causes a greater measure of suffering overall."

He explained that in 1990, a committee of doctors predicted the decriminalization of euthanasia would lead to "grave and lethal new forms of fraud, abuse, coercion and discrimination against the disabled, poor, elderly and minorities; deadly forms of coercion by insurers and faithless family members; corrosion of the doctor-patient relationship; an eventual shift to nonvoluntary and involuntary euthanasia; and widespread neglect of treatment for mental illness and pain management."

Most, if not all, of these claims can be verified in countries and states that have decriminalized assisted suicide.

"I chose to become a physician because I wanted to make a difference in peoples' lives," Callister says in the video. "We have great hospice care; and we are in a day and age where there is no reason someone should be in pain when they die," he said in a review of the proposed law in Nevada.

"I hear the horror stories of people suffering at the end, and frankly my response is, 'Sorry you didn't have a different doctor,'" he adds.

EVALUATING THE AUTHOR'S ARGUMENTS:

Viewpoint author Anita Carey argues that physician-assisted suicide laws lead to abuse. The author gives a few examples of cases where this abuse appears. Does the author provide enough information to conclude that abuse is widespread? What evidence is given to show that legal euthanasia will lead to nonvoluntary euthanasia? What more might you like to know?

Viewpoint 2

Money Makes a Difference, and That's Okay

"There is nothing inherently wrong in having an economic motive, among others, for one's behavior."

Maxwell J. Mehlman

In the following viewpoint, Maxwell J. Mehlman considers whether the cost of end-of-life care might cause patients to choose physician-assisted death instead. Economic pressure could come from several sources. Doctors, hospitals, and insurance plans might see physician-assisted death as a way to save money. Family members might prefer a quicker death, because then they don't have to spend their money on healthcare. The patient may feel guilty for taking expensive end-of-life care instead of dying quickly. Mehlman argues that people have the right to consider finances in end-of-life decisions. If poverty pressures them into choosing physician-assisted death, this might seem unfair. Yet a better answer would be to address poverty rather than denying the patient legal physician-assisted death, in this author's view. Maxwell J. Mehlman is a professor of law and biomedical ethics at Case Western Reserve University.

"Economic Motives for Physician-Assisted Suicide," by Maxwell J. Mehlman, InterMDnet Corporation, February 1, 2000.

AS YOU READ, CONSIDER THE FOLLOWING QUESTIONS:

1. Why might elderly family members worry about being an economic burden on their families?
2. How can families suffer financially when a member without health care is at the end of their life?
3. How does the author compare rich and poor patients at the end of their lives?

The debate about physician-assisted suicide is replete with concern over the role of economic factors. Justice Rehnquist, writing for a majority of the Supreme Court in *Washington v. Glucksberg*, noted the state's interest in protecting patients from "the real risk of subtle coercion and undue influence in end-of-life situations," particularly those patients "whose autonomy and well-being are already compromised by poverty." Rehnquist went on to object that, "[i]f physician-assisted suicide were permitted, many might resort to it to spare their families the substantial financial burden of end-of-life health-care costs." Justice Souter, in his concurrence, pointed out that "[p]hysicians, and their hospitals, have their own financial incentives, too, in this new age of managed care."

These concerns are shared by many scholars. The New York State Task Force on Life and the Law warns that "patients may be pressured to consent to euthanasia when their care is expensive or burdensome to others." Susan Wolf urges us to "consider the dangers of assisted suicide in the context of managed care." Nancy Osgood laments ageism in America which may lead older people to seek assisted suicide rather than become "an economic burden on younger members." John Kilner observes that, "if choosing death becomes a socially accepted alternative, then patients needing much care may begin to consider themselves selfish merely for choosing to live." "The very autonomy sought to be exercised [by permitting physician-assisted suicide] cannot be invoked if it is only allowed to be considered in a medical environment where the primary source of assisted suicide advice comes from physicians with economic interests that could objectively be at odds with those of the patient," states one student law review note entitled "Undue Economic Influence on Physician-Assisted Suicide." Another note objecting to physician-assisted suicide declares simply that, "[a]mong the many factors that influence America's health care decisions, money is the most invidious."

The Economic Objections to Physician-Assisted Suicide Fall into Three Categories

First, it is feared that physicians and other health care providers, such as hospitals and managed care organizations, faced with financial incentives to reduce health care spending, will pressure patients to request assisted suicide. Managed care plans often are financed with employer self-insured funds or with premiums paid by employers (together, in most cases, with employees). The managed care plan has an incentive to hold down spending in either case: to save employers money or to retain a profit by spending less than the amount of premiums. Managed care plans, in turn, employ various methods to encourage physicians to limit spending on plan enrollees. These techniques range from profit-sharing bonuses and risk-sharing arrangements (in which, typically. a portion of the physician's fee is withheld and returned only upon satisfactory evidence of the physician's fiscal frugality) to capitation (in which the physician is paid a fixed amount per enrollee per month, making the physician's economic incentives equivalent to those of a premium-financed plan). Confronted with these financial pressures, physicians may turn to assisted suicide as a means of reducing the costs of caring for enrollees.

Physicians also may feel that they must represent the interests of society in encouraging patients to choose less costly alternatives. Physicians may see themselves as instruments of "bedside" health care rationing. They may favor assisted suicide, particularly for older patients, in line with the beliefs of those like Daniel Callahan who think that the elderly have enjoyed enough of the resources of society and should make way for the young.

Hospitals are under economic constraints similar to managed care plans. In some cases, the hospital actually may be part of a managed care plan. In other cases, such as under Medicare, the hospital may be paid a fixed amount for a patient regardless of how long the

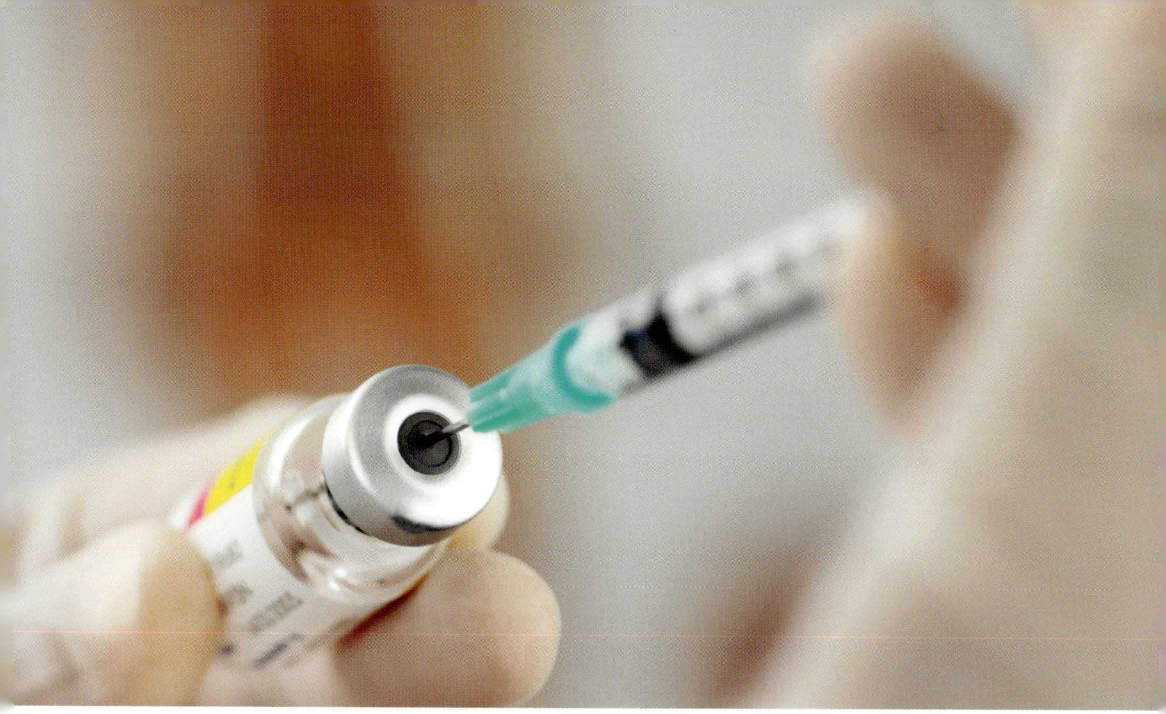

It's not hard to imagine a future in which poorer patients choose physician-assisted suicide as a way to spare their families and society economically.

patient stays in the hospital or what services the patient receives. This may lead hospital administrators to encourage their medical staffs to recommend physician-assisted suicide to hospital in-patients.

The second type of economic objection to physician-assisted suicide focuses on the role of the patient's family. Families, it is feared, may pressure patients to choose assisted suicide to avoid spending money that the patient otherwise could leave to the family. Or, family members may exert pressure because they are spending too much of their own money.

Finally, even without overt pressure from others, patients may opt for assisted suicide to save money. They may feel it is their duty to their loved-ones. They may feel they owe it to society.

Given the likely economic impact of assisted suicide, these fears arguably are worth taking seriously. Emanuel and Battin estimate that legalizing physician-assisted suicide could save each year as much as $627 million in the United States. While, as they point out, this is less than .1 percent of total annual US health care spending, the savings for an individual health plan or provider institution could be substantial enough to cause them to exert pressure on patients, either directly or through patients' physicians or families. Emanuel and Battin calculate, for example, that a large managed care plan (with 1.7 million enrollees) would save $3.3 million a year if the expected number of patients (351) chose physician-assisted suicide. The economic impact on the patient's family is likely to be even more dramatic, particularly if the patient lacks health insurance. According to Emanuel and Battin, the average family of such a patient could save $20,000 if the patient chose physician-assisted suicide. Finally, studies, not surprisingly, show that terminally-ill patients already take the costs and burdens of their care into account in making end-of-life treatment decisions; they are likely to be even more sensitive to these considerations if they perceive physician-assisted suicide as a more attractive alternative to currently available ways of dying.

The fears that physicians and other health care providers, families and patients themselves may favor assisted suicide for economic reasons, therefore, seem real. The question, however, is whether or not they should be fears.

Let's consider the third category of concerns: that patients, on their own initiative and without pressure from others, may take financial considerations into account in choosing physician-assisted suicide. Is there something necessarily improper about this? Or, more to the point, is there something so improper about this that we ought to deny that person the right to do so lawfully, by making physician-assisted suicide illegal?

Are Economic Motives for Physician-Assisted Suicide Inherently Unacceptable?

Suppose the patient choosing physician-assisted suicide is wealthy and fits whatever medical criteria are required to be a candidate. One motivation for her choice is that she wishes to leave her wealth to her family rather than to spend any more of it on her health care. But, apart from this consideration, she would not want to live anyway.

It is difficult to imagine that we would deny physician-assisted suicide to this person solely because she is taking economic considerations into account in making her decision. There is nothing inherently wrong in having an economic motive, among others, for one's behavior.

Suppose, instead, that the wealthy patient would want to go on living, but for her desire to leave her wealth to her family rather than spending any more of it on her health care. In other words, economic considerations are what tip the scales for this patient in favor of physician-assisted suicide. It is still difficult to accept that the patient's economic motivation alone should disqualify her from carrying out her wish. We may disagree with this person's decision. We may even question her competence in choosing to die in order to leave more money to her family when it already would receive a great deal of money even if she went on living. But a competent patient's right to autonomous decision-making undoubtedly extends this far.

Now suppose instead that the patient is poor, or at least significantly less well-off than the patient in the previous example. Unlike the wealthy patient for whom physician-assisted suicide may make no more difference than being able to leave another luxury automobile or two to her heirs, the poorer patient who goes on living faces the prospect of not being able to leave her family enough to live on decently.

This clearly is a more disturbing scenario, at least if we assume that the patient is poorer through no fault of her own. (Of course, that may not be the case: The patient may have less money because she gambled it away, or took expensive vacations, or chose to have a large family. Even then, we may feel sorry for the patient, just as we might feel sorry for the patient who was dying of lung cancer because she smoked cigarettes.) There is something morally wrong with someone being in such a situation. We ought to object to it and to a society that places people in such a predicament. We ought to work tirelessly to achieve a better social system. But, in the meantime, should we deny the poorer patient the ability to make her choice? Indeed, some might say that the poorer patient's ability to choose physician-assisted suicide is all the more valuable to her because of her predicament that, precisely because so much more is at stake for their families, it is more important for this option to be available to poorer patients than to richer ones.

The problem with this reasoning might seem to be that the poorer the patient, the less options that she has. If she is sufficiently poor, the patient may feel that she has no option but physician-assisted suicide,

Fast Fact

Ezekiel J. Emanuel and Margaret P. Battin reported on the expected cost savings from physician-assisted suicide. Families without insurance could save up to $20,000 if the patient chose physician-assisted suicide at the earliest possible point.

that her family's financial predicament is so dire that she has no real choice at all. In this case, we might object that, in contrast to the wealthy patient, the poorer patient's decision simply is not voluntary.

But consider the patient who chooses physician-assisted suicide to escape intractable pain, or indignity and loss of control, or simply the prospect of a lingering demise and who faces these conditions through no fault of her own. Like the poorer patient, this patient, too, faces a truly "tragic choice," to borrow a term from Calabresi and Bobbitt. Her dilemma moves us deeply. Her predicament, by depriving her of a viable alternative, may seem to deny her a voluntary choice. But does denying her the option of physician-assisted suicide improve her condition in any way?

The Same Seems True of Denying Physician-Assisted Suicide to The Poorer Patient

The two types of patients—the one facing the Hobson's choice of unbearable suffering or death, the other the Scylla of death or the Charybdis of familial impoverishment—are in morally equivalent circumstances. One seeks to be free of oppressive pain, the other of economic oppression. The plight of the poorer patient profoundly affects us.

We redouble our efforts to create a more just society. We might even take up a collection. But allowing these patients to obtain physician-assisted suicide may, in the end, allow them to make the best of a bad situation.

If, nevertheless, we deny them this option, we can have only two reasons. First, we could take the position that economic constraints are fundamentally improper grounds for making this kind of decision. In the context of the poorer patient, as in the case of the wealthy patient, this position is unpersuasive. Second, we could object that by giving these patients a way out of their predicament—albeit a distasteful one—physician-assisted suicide would impair our efforts to achieve a more just society. For example, it could deflect us from research on better types of end-of-life care. But it seems unfair to force the poorer patient to endure in order to benefit future patients. In any event, it can be argued that permitting poorer patients to avail themselves of physician-assisted suicide for economic reasons and dramatizing their plight is the most effective way to promote social change.

If that is so, then there is no convincing reason why a patient who is acting completely on her own initiative, whether she be rich or poor, should be denied physician-assisted suicide because her decision turns, in whole or in part, on economic factors. If there remains a valid objection to economic motivations for physician-assisted suicide, it must stem from the concern that the patient is not acting completely on her own initiative but under pressure from others, from health care providers and managed care organizations, or from their families.

EVALUATING THE AUTHOR'S ARGUMENTS:

Viewpoint author Maxwell J. Mehlman argues that patients have the right to consider finances when choosing how to end their lives. When might finances come into play? Do you think a patient has a right to consider money in making their decision in how to end their life? Do they have an obligation to consider money? What are the advantages and disadvantages when finances affect end-of-life care?

Viewpoint 3

Disabled People Fear Assisted Suicide

"All I see is a system which divides lives, offering suicide prevention to some, and euthanasia to others."

Jamie Hale

In the following viewpoint, Jamie Hale argues that legalizing physician-assisted death could harm people with disabilities. Many people who choose assisted suicide fear being a burden on their family, friends, or caregivers. That is a common fear among people with disabilities. They may not be able to get the care they need. Assisted suicide could appear to be the only way to solve their problems. Instead, the author suggests that health services should be better funded. She argues that mental illness can make people want to choose death at some points, but they may later be glad for life. Jamie Hale is a British poet, artist, and activist for people with disabilities. This article refers to the situation in the United Kingdom. NHS stands for National Health Service, government-funded medical and health-care services provided to everyone living in the UK.

"We're Told We Are a Burden. No Wonder Disabled People Fear Assisted Suicide," by Jamie Hale, Guardian News and Media Limited, June 1, 2018. Reprinted by permission.

AS YOU READ, CONSIDER THE FOLLOWING QUESTIONS:

1. Why is it difficult to determine when someone has less than six months to live?
2. How does poor health service funding affect people with disabilities?
3. Why might someone wish for death at one point but later appreciate life?

Opposition to assisted suicide—also called assisted dying—is characterised as being the preserve of the religious, stuffy and outdated, like religious opposition to gay marriage and abortion. In reality, some of the loudest voices opposing it are those of people with disabilities—because we have the most to fear. A poll done by Scope (a disability charity) showed that the majority of disabled people (64%) were concerned about moves to legalise assisted suicide.

Arguments around the legality of suicide and the right to refuse treatment are often conflated with assisted suicide. Suicide is legal, and there is already a right to refuse treatment. People with mental capacity can also create an advance directive to ensure their wish to refuse treatment is respected in future. This leaves people often able to die on their own terms. What assisted dying advocates are requesting is to create a system in which it is legally and morally permissible for people to engage in a deliberate action designed to end someone else's life.

There are two main models for assisted suicide legislation: the American (Oregon), and the European (Belgium and the Netherlands). The laws in Oregon restrict assisted suicide to those who are terminally ill, with less than six months to live. The number of people dying this way has increased from 15 in 1998 to 143 in 2017. There is no obligation to establish whether the petitioner has a treatable mental health problem underlying their desire to die. Nor is there one to ensure that they are not under pressure from another person. It is difficult to even establish life expectancy. Jane Campbell—the former commissioner of the Equality and Human Rights Commission—has spoken about fluctuations in her life expectancy and when it affects eligibility for assisted suicide, the stakes would be high.

People with disabilities may worry that they will be pressured into physician-assisted suicide if they are considered a burden to society.

Some 5% of people in Oregon dying by assisted suicide cited financial pressures as a cause. Meanwhile, the number citing being a "burden on family/friends/caregivers" increased from 13% in 1998 to 55% in 2017. This tallies with Scope's research that the majority of people with disabilities are concerned that legalising assisted suicide might lead to disabled people choosing it in order not to be a burden on others.

Under austerity people who are disabled, ill or elderly are constantly taught that funding our health and social care is a burden—that we are inherently a burden. I am given so little of the social care I need that I am forced to rely on unpaid care from friends to survive—and more than 10% of the population are providing unpaid care. Legalising assisted suicide may cover these cracks but only by ending our lives. In the US, insurance companies are refusing to cover the costs of treatments, while offering to pay for assisted suicide—which quickly becomes a useful cost-saving measure.

Fast Fact

According to the CDC, one in four US adults has a disability that impacts major life activities. The most common involves mobility. People living below the poverty level have much higher rates of disability.

In Belgium euthanasia for "unbearable psychological suffering" is legal. Psychiatrists are tasked both with preventing suicide, and acting as the gatekeepers to euthanasia. Even the architect of Belgium's assisted suicide legislation, Wim Distelmans, is concerned that people are being offered assisted suicide under this legislation too liberally while treatment options remain. As I know, mental illness can feel controlling, pervasive and hopeless—yet now the clouds have lifted, I am happy still to be alive.

Advocates for assisted suicide argue for the existence of an advance directive so people, with dementia for example, could decide to have their life ended were they to lose mental capacity. In the Netherlands, a doctor was cleared after having the family of a woman with dementia hold her down so he could give her the lethal injection. Her refusal of euthanasia in the present day was weighed against her historical desires, and she died.

Society's priority should be to assist us to live, not to die. Provide a free social care system funded by progressive taxation that allows us to be productive, active community members. Increase NHS funding. Cut waiting lists—there are currently 4 million people awaiting treatment. Fund wheelchairs and assistive technology. Root out the disableism that leads two-thirds of people with disabilities to think that we're seen as a burden on society. Only then can you come back to me and tell me that assisted suicide is no risk to disabled people.

I can envisage no safeguards that would prevent people being pressured into ending their lives, by interpersonal, financial or social means. All I see is a system which divides lives, offering suicide prevention to some, and euthanasia to others. When I am low and feel I cannot go on with life as a disabled adult, those around me support me, affirm that my life has meaning, and help me continue to survive. Yes, my suffering is sometimes unbearable, but the faith my loved ones have in me makes me able to bear it. Don't take that away, by legitimising assisted suicide as the right, and gracious choice.

EVALUATING THE AUTHOR'S ARGUMENTS:

In this viewpoint author Jamie Hale argues that having physician-assisted death as a legal option could pressure people with disabilities to choose that option. How common do you think this problem would be? What alternatives could society offer to people with disabilities? How likely is that to happen?

Viewpoint 4

Expand Palliative Care Instead

"A much better option than assisted suicide is the further expansion and improvement of hospices and care facilities for those with incurable conditions."

Life Charity

In the following viewpoint, Life Charity argues that all intentional killing is wrong and should be prohibited. The authors argue that instead of trying to legalize physician-assisted death, the focus should be on providing palliative care. Like some previous viewpoints, this organization worries that legal physician-assisted death could spread too far. Doctors could abuse the law by ignoring patient requests. More people could demand a right to die, for ever-expanding reasons. Life Charity is a pro-life educational and caring charity based in the UK.

AS YOU READ, CONSIDER THE FOLLOWING QUESTIONS:

1. What is hospice?
2. How do most disability rights groups feel about legal physician-assisted death?
3. How does the presumption against killing protect doctors and patients, according to the article?

"Assisted Suicide and the Hospice Alternative," Life Charity, November 30, 2016. Reprinted by permission.

Our position is not vitalist. We do not think that all life must always be preserved at any cost. We do, however, agree with the current legal prohibition on all intentional killing and specifically with the ban on assisted suicide contained in the 1961 Suicide Act. We believe that intentional killing is always wrong—though sometimes understandable—and that the consequences of legal assisted suicide would be disastrous. A much better option than assisted suicide, in our view, is the further expansion and improvement of hospices and care facilities for those with incurable conditions.

Palliative Care

Britain is a world leader in palliative care and was among the first nations in the world to build up a systematic network of hospices where people coming to the end of their lives could be looked after with dignity and in comfort. More detailed information on the history of the hospice movement and its current workings can be found on the website of St Christopher's Hospice, which was founded by Dame Cicely Saunders, one of the pioneers of palliative care in the UK.

Dame Cicely Saunders had the idea for a huge expansion of good-quality care for the dying in the years immediately following the Second World War, after her experiences nursing men injured in the conflict. At that time care for people who were dying, and were beyond any further medical help, was highly inadequate. Dame Cicely transformed that situation with the insight that the last weeks and months of life were just as important as the rest of a person's life. Every individual was important; everyone's dignity was to be respected; there was no such thing as a life worth living, and the traditional medical prohibition on intentional killing must not be infringed for the good of all society.

Looking at Precedent

A serious problem with assisted suicide is that once we have admitted into law the principle that some patients can be intentionally killed, it is very difficult to control the wider application of that principle.

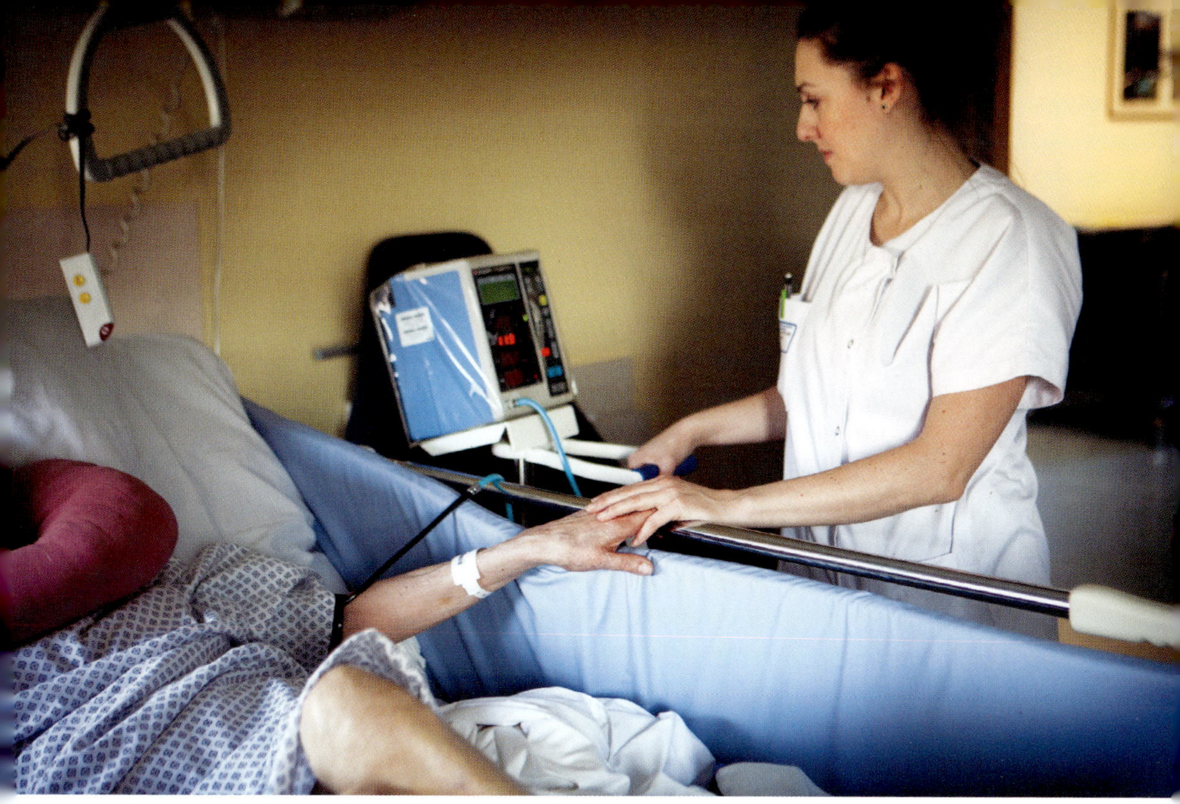

Many people believe that palliative care is the best way to achieve death with dignity.

This is because of way that the law works—we see this by looking at precedent. That is exactly what has happened, for instance, in the Netherlands. Assisted suicide has gone from being an option for a few people in very severe pain to being offered to teenagers with depression and people who have nothing physically wrong with them but are "tired of life", and non-responsive patients who have not made any request to be killed. In the Netherlands, the movement towards widespread legal assisted suicide began with a small number of individual hard cases that came before the courts.

As Professor John Keown, one of the world's leading experts on medical ethics, has written (in his 2006 work Considering Physician-Assisted Suicide):

> *The Dutch experience has been one of widespread abuse perpetrated by doctors with virtual impunity ... since 1984 the law requiring a request by the patient has been ignored in many thousands of cases ... cases of euthanasia have been illegally covered up by doctors.*

> **FAST FACT**
>
> **According to the World Health Organization, palliative care "affirms life and regards dying as a normal process." It does not attempt to either hasten or postpone death. It addresses physical, psychological, and spiritual aspects for the patient.**

If the courts granted requests for assisted suicide, it would not be long before another, similar case came before the courts, using a particular case as precedent. And that case would be followed by more and more cases, all arguing along the lines of "if he/she can do it, why can't I?"

It is in that sense that any court victory allowing assisted suicide would "open the floodgates"; it establishes the principle in medical law that it can sometimes be in a patient's best interests to be killed.

It is very difficult for this idea to co-exist with the ideals of palliative care for the dying, as we see from the relative inadequacy of end-of-life care in countries that have introduced some forms of legal euthanasia.

Endangering the Vulnerable

When we talk about endangering the vulnerable, what we are talking about is a medical and legal culture where it becomes expected that the response to disability and suffering and difficulties of old age. It is worth noting that nearly all groups that promote and safeguard the rights of people with disabilities and are opposed to any legalisation of assisted suicide. Indeed, every major disabled organisation in the country is either opposed to assisted suicide or extremely concerned about its effects on people with disabilities, for example:

- Disability Rights UK (a merger of RADAR, the Disability Alliance and the National Centre for Independent Living) ; SCOPE; the UK Disabled People's Council; Not Dead Yet UK.
- The organisation Age UK (a merger of Help The Aged and Age Concern) is opposed, as are almost all the major medical bodies, e.g. the British Medical Association, the Royal

College of Physicians and the Royal College of General Practitioners.

Protecting Doctors and Patients

At the moment the presumption is always against intentional killing. This is a form of protection for both doctors and patients. Patients do not have to worry about their lives becoming seen as a burden, or being a waste of resources. This latter point is especially important, as there is going to be a great deal of financial pressure on the NHS for the foreseeable future. Ending someone's life is cheap. Looking after a very sick person is not. If the law is changed so that killing becomes a treatment option, in the long run there must be a serious concern that financial considerations would come into play, in the form of (perhaps unconscious) psychological pressure on patients, families, doctors and hospital administrators.

As noted above, we do not think all human life should always be preserved at any cost in all circumstances. It is not ethically wrong to discontinue a medical treatment that has become over-burdensome or futile. The crucial distinction between, on the one hand, intentionally ending life, and on the other, withdrawing treatments that are no longer justified, is recognised in both ethics and law. There is, for example, a well-established right to refuse treatment for mentally competent patients, but this right has never been taken by the courts to mean that there is a right to be euthanised, just as the European Court of Human Rights has never found a right to die in European human rights law.

EVALUATING THE AUTHOR'S ARGUMENTS:

This viewpoint's author, Life Charity, argues that we should focus on palliative care rather than physician-assisted death. Viewpoints 1 and 2 in Chapter 2 claim that palliative care is not always available, does not always work when it is available, and does not always keep people from choosing to end their lives. Do you think physician-assisted death and palliative care are in opposition? Why or why not? If not, can palliative care be expanded at the same time that physician-assisted death is legalized?

Viewpoint
5

"For the first time in history, we have developed a space where people move towards death while we are touching them and they are in our midst."

Physician-Assisted Death Is Better Than Suicide

Christopher de Bellaigue

In the following excerpted viewpoint, Christopher de Bellaigue explores what it means to end one's life through physician-assisted death. He quotes a doctor who notes that this process is very different from committing suicide in private without the knowledge of your family. The author then interviews additional people who share personal stories about their experiences with physician-assisted death and suicide. This reporting takes place in the Netherlands, whose people are known as the Dutch. In the Netherlands, the term *euthanasia* is used both when medical professionals administer a lethal injection and when doctors provide drugs that patients can take to end their life. Christopher de Bellaigue is a journalist and author who has covered the Middle East and South Asia since 1994. His latest book is *The Islamic Enlightenment: The Modern Struggle Between Faith and Reason*.

"Death on Demand: Has Euthanasia Gone Too Far?" by Christopher de Bellaigue, Guardian News and Media Limited, January 18, 2019. Reprinted by permission.

AS YOU READ, CONSIDER THE FOLLOWING QUESTIONS:

1. How is physician-assisted death different from committing suicide in secret?
2. What does the author mean by "consensual" suicide?
3. Why might doctors who are willing to perform physician-assisted suicide still refuse when it comes to mentally ill people who are not elderly?

Last year a Dutch doctor called Bert Keizer was summoned to the house of a man dying of lung cancer, in order to end his life. When Keizer and the nurse who was to assist him arrived, they found around 35 people gathered around the dying man's bed. "They were drinking and guffawing and crying," Keizer told me when I met him in Amsterdam recently. "It was boisterous. And I thought: 'How am I going to cleave the waters?' But the man knew exactly what to do. Suddenly he said, 'OK, guys!' and everyone understood. Everyone fell silent. The very small children were taken out of the room and I gave him his injection. I could have kissed him, because I wouldn't have known how to break up the party."

Keizer is one of around 60 physicians on the books of the Levenseindekliniek, or End of Life Clinic, which matches doctors willing to perform euthanasia with patients seeking an end to their lives, and which was responsible for the euthanasia of some 750 people in 2017. For Keizer, who was a philosopher before studying medicine, the advent of widespread access to euthanasia represents a new era. "For the first time in history," he told me, "we have developed a space where people move towards death while we are touching them and they are in our midst. That's completely different from killing yourself when your wife's out shopping and the kids are at school and you hang yourself in the library—which is the most horrible way of doing it, because the wound never heals. The fact that you are a person means that you are linked to other people. And we have found a bearable way of severing that link, not by a natural death, but by a self-willed ending. It's a very special thing."

[...]

Bert Keizer carried out his first euthanasia in 1984. Back then, when he was working as a doctor in a care home, ending the life of a desperately ill person at their request was illegal, even if prosecutions were rare. When a retired shoemaker called Antonius Albertus, who was dying of lung cancer, asked to be put out of his misery, Keizer found that two sides of himself—the law-abiding doctor and the altruist—were at odds.

"Antonius wasn't in pain," Keizer told me, "but he had that particular exhaustion that every oncologist knows, a harrowing exhaustion, and I saw him dwindle before me." In the event, Keizer, who as an 11-year-old watched his mother suffer an excruciating death from liver disease, went with the altruist. He injected 40mg of Valium into Antonius—enough to put him in a coma—then gave him the anti-respiratory drug that ended his life.

Keizer was not investigated after reporting an unnatural death at his own hand, and his career did not suffer as he feared it might. But what, I asked him, had prompted him to break the law, and violate a principle—the preservation of life—that has defined medical ethics since Hippocrates? Keizer paused to brush away a spider that had crawled uninvited on to my shoulder. "It was something very selfish," he replied. "If ever I was in his situation, asking for death, I would want people to listen to me, and not say, 'It cannot be done because of the law or the Bible.'"

Over the past few decades the Bible has been increasingly sidelined, and the law has vindicated the young doctor who put Antonius to sleep. As people got used to the new law, the number of Dutch people being euthanised began to rise sharply, from under 2,000 in 2007 to almost 6,600 in 2017. (Around the same number are estimated to have had their euthanasia request turned down as not conforming with the legal requirements.) Also in 2017, some 1,900 Dutch people killed themselves, while the number of people who died under palliative sedation—in theory, succumbing to their illness while cocooned from physical discomfort, but in practice often dying of dehydration while unconscious—hit an astonishing 32,000. Altogether, well over a quarter of all deaths in 2017 in the Netherlands were induced.

[...]

Tens of thousands of protesters demonstrated outside the Hague as Parliament debated the legalization of euthanasia. A law passed in 2001 allows physician-assisted suicide in accordance with specific criteria.

In November 2016, Monique and Bert de Gooijer, a couple from Tilburg, became minor celebrities when a regional paper, the Brabants Dagblad, devoted an entire issue to the euthanasia of their son, an obese, darkly humorous, profoundly disturbed 38-year-old called Eelco. His euthanasia was one of the first high-profile cases involving a young person suffering from mental illness. Of the hundreds of reactions the newspaper received, most of them supportive, the one that made the biggest impression on the de Gooijers came from a woman whose daughter had gone out one day, taking the empty bottles to the store, and walked in front of a train. "She envied us," Monique told me as I sat with her and Bert in their front room, "because she didn't know why her daughter had done it. She said: 'You were able to ask Eelco every question you had. I have only questions.'"

Privately, even surreptitiously undertaken, suicide leaves behind shattered lives. Even when it goes according to plan, someone finds a body. That openly discussed euthanasia can cushion or even obviate much of this hurt is something I hadn't really considered before meeting the de Gooijers. Nor had I fully savoured the irony that suicide, with its high risk of failure and collateral damage, was illegal across Europe until a few decades ago, while euthanasia, with its apparently more benign—at least, more manageable—consequences, remains illegal in most countries.

Whatever the act of killing a physically healthy young man tells us about Dutch views of human wellbeing, the demise of Eelco de Gooijer didn't traumatise a train driver or a weekender fishing in a canal. Eelco was euthanised only after long thought and discussions with his family. He enjoyed a good laugh with the undertaker who had come to take his measurements for a super-size coffin. He was able to say farewell to everyone who loved him, and he died, as Monique and Bert assured me, at peace. There might be a word for this kind of suicide, the kind that is acceptable to all parties. Call it consensual.

"You try to make your child happy," Monique said in her matter-of-fact way, "but Eelco wasn't happy in life. He wanted to stop suffering, and death was the only way." Eelco came of age just as euthanasia was being legalised. After years of being examined by psychiatrists who made multiple diagnoses and prescribed a variety of ineffective remedies, he began pestering the doctors of Tilburg to end his life.

[…]

A category of euthanasia request that Dutch doctors commonly reject is that of a mentally ill person whose desire to die could be interpreted as a symptom of a treatable psychiatric disease—Eelco de Gooijer, in other words. Eelco was turned down by two doctors in Tilburg; one of them balked at doing the deed because she was pregnant. In desperation, Eelco turned to the Levenseindekliniek. With its ideological commitment to euthanasia and cadre of specialist doctors, it has done much to help widen the scope of the practice, and one of its teams ended Eelco's misery on 23 November 2016. A second team from the same clinic killed another psychologically disturbed youngster, Aurelia Brouwers, early last year.

FAST FACT

The Netherlands has one of the broadest legal options for physician-assisted death. The patient's request must be informed, voluntary, and well considered. The doctor must be satisfied that the patient has unbearable suffering, without prospect of improvement, and that there is no reasonable alternative to address it.

Ideally euthanasia is a structure with three struts: patient, doctor and the patient's loved ones. In the case of Eelco de Gooijer, the struts were sturdy and aligned. Eelco's death was accomplished with compassion, circumspection and scrupulous regard for the feelings of all concerned. It's little wonder that the Dutch Voluntary Euthanasia Society, or NVVE, vaunts it as an example of euthanasia at its best.

After leaving the de Gooijers, I drove northwards, bisecting hectares of plant nurseries, skirting Tesla's European factory, to a conference organised by the NVVE. Apart from being the parent organisation of the Levenseindekliek, the NVVE, with its membership of 170,000 (bigger than any Dutch political party) and rolling programme of public meetings, is one of the most powerful interest groups in the Netherlands. The conference that day was aimed at tackling psychiatrists' well known opposition to euthanasia for psychiatric cases—in effect, trying to break down the considerable opposition that remains among psychiatrists to euthanising disturbed youngsters like Eelco and Aurelia.

[…]

Over coffee I was introduced to Steven Pleiter, the director of the Levenseindekliniek. We went outside and basked in the early October sun as he described the "shift in mindset" he is trying to achieve. Choosing his words with care, Pleiter said he hoped that in future doctors will feel more confident accommodating demands for "the most complex varieties of euthanasia, like psychiatric illnesses and dementia"—not through a change in the law, he added, but through a kind of "acceptance … that grows and grows over the years". When I asked him if he understood the scruples of those doctors who refuse to perform euthanasia because they entered their profession in order to save lives, he replied: "If the situation is unbearable and there is no prospect of improvement, and euthanasia is an option, it would be almost unethical [of a doctor] not to help that person."

[...]

EVALUATING THE AUTHOR'S ARGUMENTS:

Viewpoint author Christopher de Bellaigue explores how suicide, committed in secret without the knowledge or approval of one's family, is different from physician-assisted death. Do you see these forms of ending one's life as different? Why or why not?

Facts About Physician-Assisted Suicide

Editor's note: These facts can be used in reports to add credibility when making important points or claims.

According to the Hastings Center, terms can be defined as follows:

Physician-assisted death—the practice of a physician providing the means for a person with decision-making capacity to take his or own life, usually with a prescription for barbiturates that patient takes himself or herself; sometimes also called physician-assisted suicide, physician aid-in-dying, and patient administered hastened death)

Euthanasia—painlessly killing or permitting the death of individuals who are ill or injured beyond hope of recovery.

Voluntary active euthanasia—hastening one's own death by use of drugs or other means, with a doctor's direct assistance.

Passive euthanasia—hastening death by withdrawing life-sustaining treatment and letting nature take its course

Involuntary euthanasia—causing or hastening the death of someone who has not asked for assistance with dying, such as a patient who has lost consciousness and is unlikely to regain it or who lacks decision-making capacity for other reasons.

Physician-assisted suicide (PAS) may also be called medical aid in dying (MAID). The terms used can evoke emotional feelings. In opinion polls, people may have a more negative reaction to "doctor assisted suicide" versus "medical aid in dying" or "right to die," due to negative feelings about the word suicide.

Physician-assisted death is sometimes separated into active or passive forms. In the active form, the patient is given something to hurry death. In the passive form, treatments that prolong life are withheld. For example, life support systems may be turned off, allowing the patient to die.

The "dying with dignity" movement claims people should be able to die on their own terms. This movement involves offering options to terminally ill patients. Those options can include physician-assisted death, suicide, refusing medical treatments, and refusing food and drink.

Laws and Opinions

In America, public opinion has been moving toward acceptance of physician-assisted death. In 1950, fewer than four in 10 people supported the practice according to a Gallup poll. By 1973, 53 percent were in favor.

In 2018, Gallup reported that 72 percent of Americans now support legal physician-assisted death. The report notes, "While support for legalized euthanasia is strong across nearly all subgroups of Americans, men, young adults, Democrats and liberals are especially likely to favor it. Support drops below a majority only among weekly churchgoers."

Physician-assisted suicide first became legal in the U.S. in 1997 under Oregon's "Death with Dignity" law. California, Colorado, Hawaii, Vermont, Washington, and the district of Columbia have adopted death with dignity acts. These laws allow terminally ill people to choose when and how they die. Montana doesn't have such a law, but end-of-life options are legal due to a court ruling. Twenty-six other states are considering legalizing assisted suicide as of 2019.

The American Medical Association provides Code of Medical Ethics Opinions both for and against physician-assisted suicide. The opposition opinion states, "Physician-assisted suicide is fundamentally incompatible with the physician's role as healer."

The AMA favorable opinion says physicians should: "Uphold standards of informed consent and inform the patient about all relevant options for treatment, including options to which the physician morally objects.

"In general, physicians should refer a patient to another physician or institution to provide treatment the physician declines to offer. When a deeply held, well-considered personal belief leads a physician also to decline to refer, the physician should offer impartial guidance to patients about how to inform themselves regarding access to desired services."

Physician-Assisted Death in Practice

Several states issue reports on their PAS programs. However, each state tracks and reports results differently. This makes it hard to compare the states or determine overall effects.

Between 1998 and 2017, 4249 prescriptions were written for PAS drugs. Two thirds of patients actually used those drugs to end their lives; the others died from their diseases. The majority were 69-89 years old, and 63 percent had cancer.

For the five states that report on their PAS programs, the total average yearly deaths due to PAS drugs was estimated at 548.7 people.

End-of-Life Alternatives to Physician-Assisted Death

Palliative care attempts to relieve suffering for patients at the end of life. According to the World Health Organization, palliative care "affirms life and regards dying as a normal process." It does not attempt to either hasten or postpone death. It addresses physical, psychological, and spiritual aspects for the patient. Palliative care also attempts to help the patient's family deal with the death.

According to the Hospice Foundation of America, hospice is "Medical care to help someone with a terminal illness live as well as possible for as long as possible, increasing quality of life." It involves a team of professionals who address the physical, mental, and spiritual concerns of the dying person and their family. Generally it is available for people with a life expectancy of six months or less. People may receive hospice services at home, in a hospital, in a nursing home, or in an assisted living center.

Organizations to Contact

The editors have compiled the following list of organizations concerned with the issues debated in this book. The descriptions are derived from materials provided by the organizations. All have publications or information available for interested readers. The list was compiled on the date of publication of the present volume; the information provided here may change. Be aware that many organizations take several weeks or longer to respond to inquiries, so allow as much time as possible for the receipt of requested materials.

Care Not Killing

6 Marshalsea Road
London, UK
contact form: www.carenotkilling.org.uk/contact/
website: www.carenotkilling.org.uk
Care Not Killing is an alliance of people and organizations based in Britain. They are in favor of palliative care and opposed to assisted suicide. The website includes news, personal stories, and ways to get involved.

Compassion and Choices

101 SW Madison Street, #8009
Portland, OR 97207
(800) 247-7421
email: scrowley@compassionandchoices.org
website: www.CompassionandChoices.org
This organization is involved in legal defense and lobbying efforts to expand right to die legislation in the United States and, to some extent, Canada. They offer consultations, assistance, and support.

Death with Dignity National Center

520 SW 6th Avenue, Suite 1220
Portland, OR 97204
(503) 228-4415

contact form: www.deathwithdignity.org/about/contact/
website: www.deathwithdignity.org/
Death with Dignity is a nonprofit organization that promotes legal physician-assisted death. Their website offers news about death with dignity laws in various states. Resources include end-of-life resources for patients and families.

Exit International

(360) 961-1333
email: contact@exitinternational.net
website: exitinternational.net/
The goal of Exit International is to "ensure that all rational adults have access to the best available information so that they may make informed decisions over when and how they die." The organization's website has links to newsletters, but some material is exclusive to members.

The Final Exit Network

P.O. Box 10071
Tallahassee, FL 32302
(866) 654-9156
email: finalexitnetworkcontact@gmail.com
website: www.FinalExitNetwork.org
The Final Exit Network educates people about end-of-life choices, and it provides volunteers to help people negotiate their death. The website lists books, newsletters, and other resources.

Not Dead Yet

497 State Street
Rochester, NY 14608
(708) 420-0539
contact form: https://notdeadyet.org/about/contact-us
website: notdeadyet.org/
The Not Dead Yet website links to national disability organizations that oppose legalization of physician-assisted death. Their Toolkit provides information on the topic from the viewpoint of disability rights.

Patients Rights Council

PO Box 760
Steubenville, OH 43952
(740) 282-3810
contact form: www.patientsrightscouncil.org/site/contact/
website: www.PatientsRightsCouncil.org

The Patients Rights Council opposes right-to-die legislation. The organization believes the healthcare industry will promote it to contain costs. Their website covers issues, laws, and news.

The Right to Die Society of Canada

145 Macdonell Avenue
Toronto, Ontario, Canada
M6R 2A4
(416) 535-0690
email: info@righttodie.ca
website: www.RighttoDie.ca

This Right to Die Society of Canada lobbies for right to die legislature in Canada and educates the public. The website has a "Researchers' Buffet" which includes pros and cons, history, definitions, and more.

The World Federation of Right to Die Societies

email: info@worldrtd.net
website: www.worldrtd.net

The World Federation of Right to Die Societies is a network of 49 right to die organizations from twenty-six countries. The organizations work "to secure or protect the rights of individuals to self-determination at the end of their lives." The website's media page provides a search function for books, newsletters, films, and other publications.

For Further Reading

Books

Brewer, Colin, ed. *I'll See Myself Out, Thank You: Thirty Personal Views in Support of Assisted Suicide*. Bloxham, UK: Skyscraper Publications, 2015. Essays cover the legal and religious issues surrounding physician-assisted death, along with personal experience stories from patients and caregivers.

Butler, Katy. *The Art of Dying Well: A Practical Guide to a Good End of Life*. New York, NY: Scribner, 2019. This is a "manual for living, aging, and dying with meaning and even joy." It includes advice for living as long as possible as well as possible.

Butler, Katy. *Knocking on Heaven's Door: The Path to a Better Way of Death*. New York, NY: Scribner, 2013. This is part memoir and part investigative reporting. The author recounts her father's lengthy illness and death, and the toll it took on her and her mother. She then explores issues surrounding death and medicine.

Gawande, Atul. *Being Mortal: Medicine and What Matters in the End*. London, UK: Picador, 2017. A surgeon examines the limitations of medicine when it comes to end-of-life care. He focuses on how people can live a good life until the end. The paperback version includes a reading group guide.

Mannix, Kathryn. *With the End in Mind: Dying, Death, and Wisdom in an Age of Denial*. New York, NY: Little, Brown and Company, 2018. A palliative care doctor shares stories from decades spent caring for the dying.

McKissock, Nina Angela. *From Sun to Sun: A Hospice Nurse Reflects on the Art of Dying*. She Writes Press, 2015. A hospice nurse describes how people of different ages have dealt with their impending deaths.

Miller, BJ and Shoshana Berger. *A Beginner's Guide to the End: Practical Advice for Living Life and Facing Death*. New York, NY: Simon & Schuster, 2019. A hospice physician shares step-by-step instructions for dealing with the end of a life. The book also includes advice for survivors.

Pappas, Demetra M. *The Euthanasia/Assisted-Suicide Debate*. Westport, CT: Greenwood, 2012. This title explores the history and politics of the modern assisted death debate. Case studies explore legal issues regarding euthanasia and assisted suicide.

Sumner, Wayne. *Physician-Assisted Death: What Everyone Needs to Know*. Oxford, UK: Oxford University Press, 2017. This title explores the movement to legalize physician-assisted death. It reviews the main arguments on both sides of the controversy.

Tisdale, Sallie. *Advice for Future Corpses (and Those Who Love Them): A Practical Perspective on Death and Dying*. New York, NY: Simon & Schuster, 2018. A nurse shares anecdotes based on her work in palliative care. She explores questions such as, "What does it mean to die a good death?"

Periodicals and Internet Sources

Callaghan, Sascha, "Should people with acute mental suffering be allowed to die?" November 14, 2014. https://theconversation.com/should-people-with-acute-mental-suffering-be-allowed-to-die-34233

Diep, Francie, "How Physician-Assisted Suicide Happens around the World," June 14, 2017. https://psmag.com/news/how-physician-assisted-suicide-happens-around-the-world

Drum, Kevin. "My Right to Die: Assisted Suicide, my family, and me." Mother Jones Magazine, Jan/Feb 2016. https://www.motherjones.com/politics/2016/01/assisted-suicide-legalization-california-kevin-drum/

Emanuel, Ezekiel J., M.D., Ph.D., and Margaret P. Battin, Ph.D. "What Are the Potential Cost Savings from Legalizing Physician-Assisted Suicide?" The New England Journal of Medicine, July 16, 1998. https://www.nejm.org/doi/10.1056/NEJM199807163390306

Grant, Matthew, "It's not all about death: conversations with patients in palliative care," November 3, 2017. https://theconversation.com/its-not-all-about-death-conversations-with-patients-in-palliative-care-82247

Jarvis, Brooke. "When I Die: An end-of-life doctor faces his own end." Harper's Magazine, April 2016.

Lee, Jae Rhim, "My Mushroom Burial Suit," TED Talk, 2011. https://www.ted.com/talks/jae_rhim_lee_my_mushroom_burial_suit

Miller, BJ, "What Really Matters At The End of Life," TED Talk, 2015. https://www.ted.com/talks/bj_miller_what_really_matters_at_the_end_of_life

Mohammed, Zaineb. "Why Americans Can't Die with Dignity: Author Katy Butler on overtreatment, end-of-life suffering, and the need for a Slow Medicine movement." Mother Jones Magazine, September 2013.

Neustatter, Angela, "Assisted dying: how does it work in a Dutch end-of-life clinic?" September 11, 2015. https://www.theguardian.com/lifeandstyle/2015/sep/11/assisted-dying-dutch-end-of-life-netherlands-unbearable-suffering

Ollove, Michael, "Palliative Sedation, an End-of-Life Practice That Is Legal Everywhere," Stateline, July 2, 2018. https://www.pewtrusts.org/en/research-and-analysis/blogs/stateline/2018/07/02/palliative-sedation-an-endoflife-practice-that-is-legal-everywhere

Phillips, Avery, "Should Assisted Suicide Be Legalized for Those in Poor Health?" February 13, 2019. https://tincture.io/should-assisted-suicide-be-legalized-for-those-in-poor-health-129f8f6844f3

"Physician-Assisted Suicide is Wrong," La Salette Communications Center. https://www.lasalette.org/reflections/727-physician-assisted-suicide-is-wrong.html

Reinberg, Steven, "Most Doctors Oppose Physician-Assisted Suicide, Poll Finds." HealthDay News, September 11, 2013. https://www.medicinenet.com/script/main/art.asp?articlekey=173522

Saul, Peter, "Let's Talk About Dying," TED Talk, 2011. https://www.ted.com/talks/peter_saul_let_s_talk_about_dying?language=en

"Should Euthanasia or Physician-Assisted Suicide Be Legal?" ProCon.org. May 15, 2018. https://euthanasia.procon.org/view.answers.php?questionID=001320

"State-by-State Physician-Assisted Suicide Statistics," ProCon.org. January 28, 2019. https://euthanasia.procon.org/view.resource.php?resourceID=006992

Thompson, Dennis, "Most Americans Agree With Right-to-Die Movement," December 5, 2014. https://consumer.healthday.com/mental-health-information-25/behavior-health-news-56/most-americans-agree-with-right-to-die-movement-694268.html

"Top 10 Pro & Con Arguments: Should euthanasia or physician-assisted suicide be legal?" ProCon.org. October 9, 2018. https://euthanasia.procon.org/view.resource.php?resourceID=000126

White, Frederick, "US doctors vote to oppose assisted suicide," June 20 2019. https://www.bioedge.org/indepth/view/us-doctors-vote-to-oppose-assisted-suicide/13108

"Would Legalizing Physician-Assisted Suicide or Voluntary Euthanasia Create a Slippery Slope to Nonvoluntary or Involuntary Euthanasia?" ProCon.org. July 9, 2018. https://euthanasia.procon.org/view.answers.php?questionID=001592

Websites

Death with Dignity (www.deathwithdignity.org)
Death with Dignity promotes legal physician-assisted death. Their website offers news about laws in various states, facts about end-of-life options, and personal stories from patients and family members.

Euthanasia.com (www.euthanasia.com)
This group opposes physician-assisted death. The website provides links to hundreds of articles about right-to-die laws and organizations that oppose those laws.

Hastings Center Bioethics Briefings (www.thehastingscenter.org/briefingbook/physician-assisted-death/)
The Hastings Center has an ethics briefing on physician-assisted death. It includes information about the debate, plus a glossary of terms.

Index

Picture Credits

Cover Goodboy Picture Company/E+/Getty Images; pp. 11, 90, 102 © AP Images; p. 14 Amelie-Benoist/BSIP/Corbis Documentary/Getty Images; p. 21 Han Lans/The Image Bank/Getty Images; p. 27 Gallup/https://news.gallup.com/poll/235145/americans-strong-support-euthanasia-persists.aspx. Downloaded Nov. 16, 2019; p. 33 Christian Science Monitor/Getty Images; p. 41 Amelie-Benoist/Corbis/Getty Images; p. 44 Stephen Smith/The Image Bank/Getty Images; p. 47 Karen Kasmauski/Corbis NX/Getty Images; p. 54 Hero Images/Getty Images; p. 58 ljubaphoto/E+/Getty Images; p. 64 Portland Press Herald/Getty Images; p. 71 Angela Wyant/The Image Bank/Getty Images; p. 74 The Independent Record/AP Images; p. 77 Reza Estakhrian/Stone/Getty Images; p. 83 TEK Image/Science Photo Library/Getty Images; p. 95 BSIP/Universal Images Group/Getty Images.